Landmark Visitors Guide

Kraków

Andrew Beattie & Tim Pepper

Andrew Beattie read geography at Mansfield College, Oxford and teaches the subject at an independent school in London. He has accompanied groups of pupils to places as diverse as Greenland and the Dead Sea, and has also travelled extensively in eastern and southern Europe, in the Middle East and in India. His most recent books are *Cairo: a cultural History* and *The Alps: a cultural History* (both Signal Books/OUP).

Tim Pepper has been writing and travelling ever since leaving Wadham College, Oxford with a degree in history. His wanderings have taken him from the deserts of North Africa to the jungles of Mexico. He presently lives in Buckinghamshire.

Andrew Beattie and Tim Pepper are the authors of another book in this series, *Landmark Visitor's Guide: Ticino, Switzerland* and also the first and second editions of a book on Syria in the *Rough Guides* series.

Published by

Landmark Publishing
Ashbourne Hall, Cokayne Ave, Ashbourne,
Derbyshire DE6 1EJ England

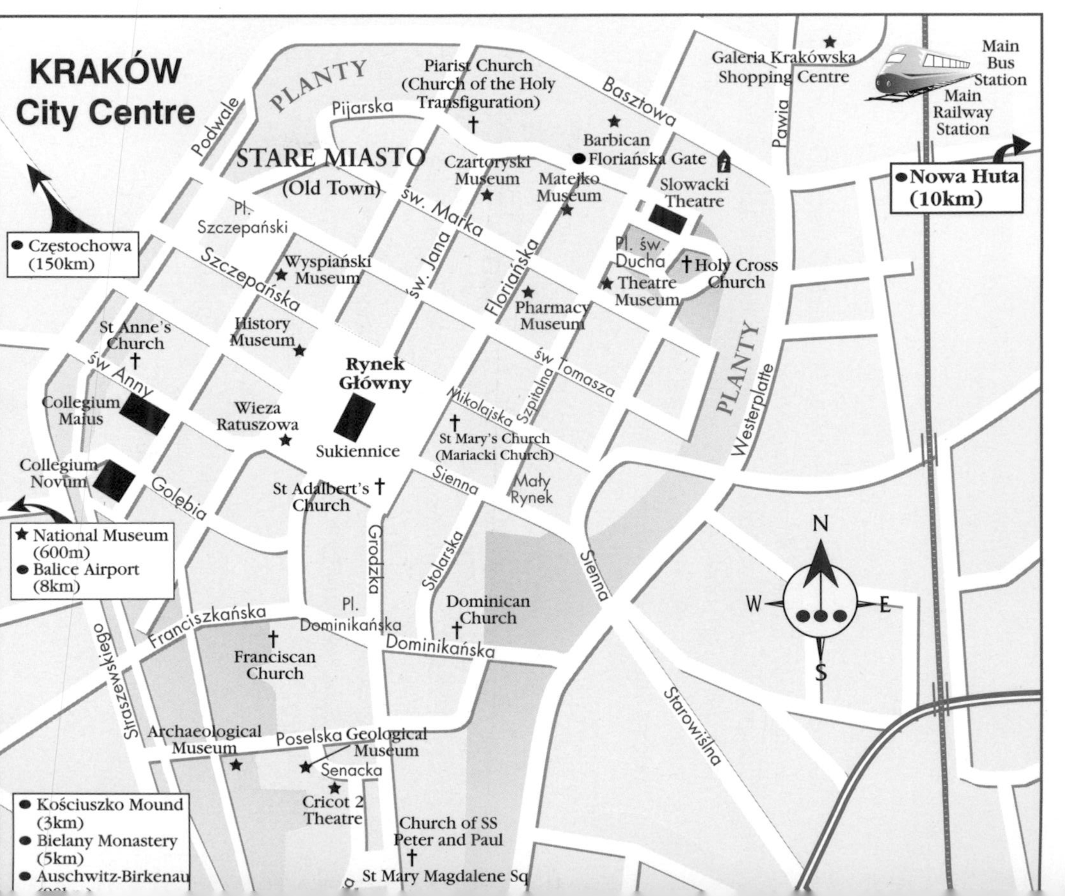

KRAKÓW
City Centre
Częstochowa (150km)
National Museum (600m)
Balice Airport (8km)
Kościuszko Mound (3km)
Bielany Monastery (5km)
Auschwitz-Birkenau
Podwale
PLANTY
Pijarska
Piarist Church (Church of the Holy Transfiguration)
Basztowa
Galeria Krakówska Shopping Centre
Main Bus Station
Main Railway Station
Pawia
Nowa Huta (10km)
STARE MIASTO (Old Town)
Czartoryski Museum
Matejko Museum
Barbican
Floriańska Gate
Slowacki Theatre
Pl. św. Ducha
Holy Cross Church
Theatre Museum
Pl. Szczepański
Szczepańska
Wyspiański Museum
św. Marka
św. Jana
Floriańska
Pharmacy Museum
St Anne's Church
św. Anny
History Museum
Rynek Główny
św. Tomasza
Szpitalna
Mikołajska
Collegium Maius
Wieża Ratuszowa
Sukiennice
St Mary's Church (Mariacki Church)
Westerplatte
Collegium Novum
Gołębia
St Adalbert's Church
Sienna
Mały Rynek
Grodzka
Stolarska
Dominican Church
Pl. Dominikańska
Dominikańska
Franciszkańska
Franciscan Church
Straszewskiego
Archaeological Museum
Poselska
Geological Museum
Senacka
Cricot 2 Theatre
Church of SS Peter and Paul
St Mary Magdalene Sq
Starowiślna
N
W
E
S

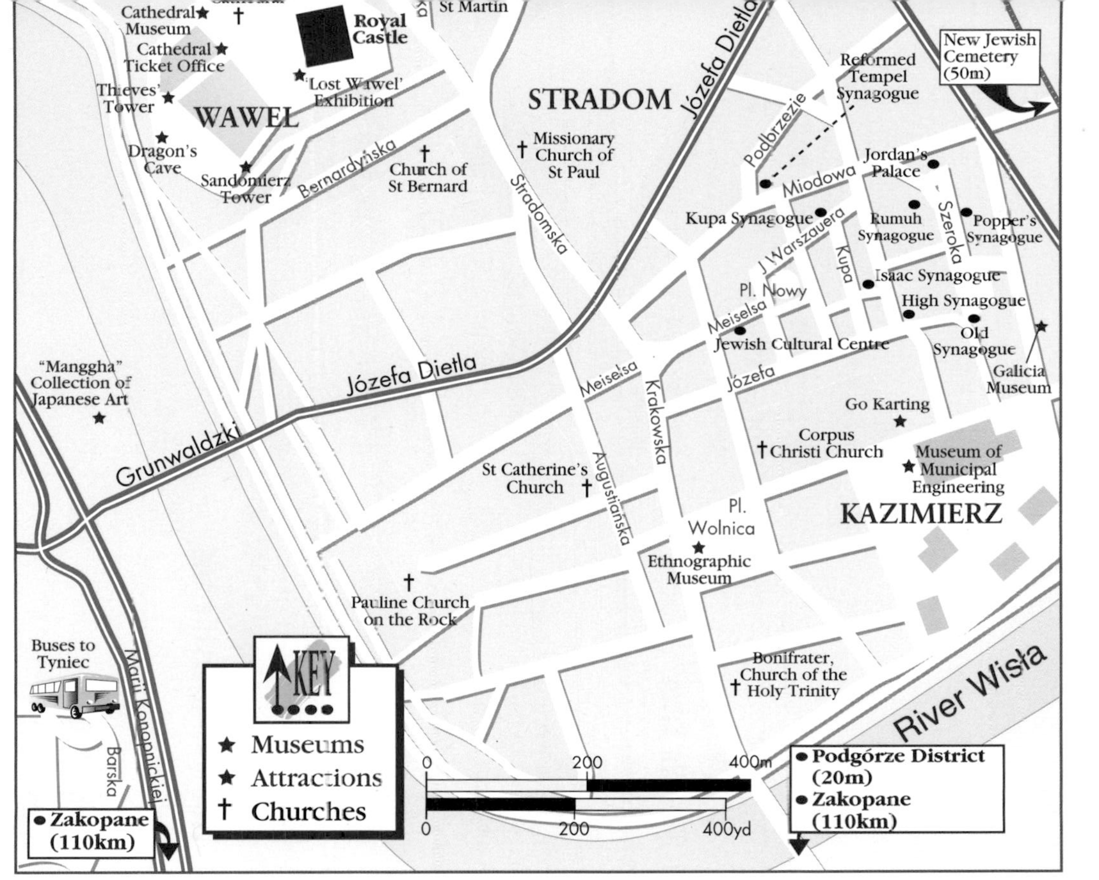

Cathedral Museum
Royal Castle
St Martin
Cathedral Ticket Office
'Lost Wawel' Exhibition
Thieves' Tower
WAWEL
Dragon's Cave
Sandomierz Tower
Bernardyńska
Church of St Bernard
STRADOM
Józefa Dietla
Missionary Church of St Paul
Stradomska
Reformed Tempel Synagogue
New Jewish Cemetery (50m)
Podbrzezie
Miodowa
Jordan's Palace
Kupa Synagogue
J. Warszauera
Rumuh Synagogue
Szeroka
Popper's Synagogue
Kupa
Isaac Synagogue
Pl. Nowy
High Synagogue
Meiselsa
Jewish Cultural Centre
Old Synagogue
Galicia Museum
"Manggha" Collection of Japanese Art
Józefa Dietla
Meiselsa
Krakowska
Józefa
Go Karting
Grunwaldzki
Corpus Christi Church
Museum of Municipal Engineering
St Catherine's Church
Augustiańska
Pl. Wolnica
KAZIMIERZ
Ethnographic Museum
Pauline Church on the Rock
Buses to Tyniec
KEY
Museums
Attractions
Churches
Bonifrater, Church of the Holy Trinity
River Wisła
Marii Konopnickiej
Barska
0
200
400m
0
200
400yd
Podgórze District (20m)
Zakopane (110km)
Zakopane (110km)

Contents

Feature Boxes

Maps

Welcome to Kraków

Left: Kraków is a city of music - given in the form of formal classical concerts, in jazz bars, at rock gigs and by street musicians
Opposite: The Cathedral on Wawel Hill

Kraków is one of the most enticing cities in Eastern Europe. The political capital of Poland for nearly six hundred years, it is still arguably the country's cultural and spiritual centre. The architectural legacy of its mercantile and political importance includes the fabulous Wawel Castle and Cathedral, St Mary's Church and the expansive main square, the Rynek Główny.

Top Tips

- Kraków is a city for walking. In the city centre you will find everything from backpacker hostels to luxury international hotels. Try to stay in one of these and enjoy the city on foot.
- The public transport system is extensive and very cheap and easy to use – once you get the hang of a few basics.
- Krakow is a city full of churches. The two largest and most important are St Mary's Church, right in the heart of the Old Town, and Wawel Cathedral, the former cathedral church of the Kings of Poland.
- Take a trip out into the suburbs or countryside and experience a very different side to Poland than the city's ancient core: ancient monasteries, pilgrimage towns, rolling countryside, mountain resorts and a salt mine all await discovery. And there are some excellent opportunities for country walks in the Wolski Forest, right on the city's doorstep.
- Away from sightseeing, spend time drinking in the atmosphere in the city's coffee bars, shopping in street markets or modern shopping complexes, browsing in bookshops, eating in restaurants serving traditional Polish food, or even taking in a visit to a concert or opera.
- To get the most out of a visit to Kraków, appreciate the fact that it is not one city, but many: a modern centre for arts and culture; an ancient mercantile centre; a university city; a former royal stronghold; an industrial city that was once at the heart of communist Poland; and a city with strong Roman Catholic and Jewish traditions. All these facets of the city can be seen by those who take time to seek out its architectural heritage.

But there's another side too to Kraków's history, one which is complex and often tragic, and which is again a result of the city lying at the centre of Europe: it is these scars - of the twentieth century which arguably leave the greatest impression on visitors, and it's impossible not to be moved by the evidence of the Nazi occupation of Kraków, which is most immediately apparent in the ruin of the former Jewish Quarter, or by the horrors of Auschwitz-Birkenau, less than an hour's drive from the city.

History

Kraków is centred around a rocky hill, Wawel (pronounced 'Vavel') situated at a bend in the River Wisła (Vistula). According to popular legend, the city was founded by a mythical king named Krak, from whom it is said to derive its name. Numerous tales and legends testify to Krak's wise and courageous leadership, and it's possible that they refer to some actual ruler, though nothing has ever been proved.

Flint tools found on Wawel Hill suggest that the place has been inhabited since prehistoric times, though, as only 30cm (12in) of soil coat the hill, it meant that all new building destroyed whatever had been there previously. Consequently, it is hard to be precise about much of Kraków's history before the first written reference to the city in 965. By then it had become an important trading town on the routes heading east from Wrocław to Lwów and Ruthenia, and north from Hungary to the Baltic.

By the tenth century Kraków had been incorporated into the lands held by the Polanie. In 966 the leader of the Polanie, Duke Mieszko I, was converted to Christianity and this is traditionally regarded as being the birth date of the Polish state. A bishopric was founded in Kraków in 1000AD and a number of important buildings were constructed on Wawel Hill, including the first version of the cathedral. Kraków was made capital of Poland in 1038, a status it retained until the early seventeenth century.

In 1241 Kraków was razed by the Mongols, a fearsomely destructive tribe from the east; the city's frightened citizens huddled on Wawel and inside the fortified Church of St Andrew to escape the carnage. Twice more these invaders devastated Kraków - in 1259-60 and 1287. In 1257 the town below Wawel was rebuilt, essentially as one finds it today, with a large main square surrounded by streets laid out in a grid pattern. It was also encircled by a fortified wall and moat, most of which was replaced in the nineteenth century by the parks which ring the inner city today.

Medieval Glory

In the early fourteenth century Wawel Cathedral became the place where Polish kings were crowned and buried; thirty-seven coronations have taken place here and all but two Polish kings are buried either under the cathedral floor or in its crypt. Kraków's commercial prosperity in this period is reflected by the number of impressive churches built (including the present day version of Wawel Cathedral) and the founding of a university in 1364 (which includes the astronomer Nicolaus Copernicus among its alumni).

Kazimierz the Great

Kazimierz (Casimir) the Great (r.1333—70) was one of Poland's most important rulers. He strengthened royal authority in Poland through the creation of a new administrative system and the unifying and codifying of the country's laws, and managed to almost double Poland's territory by buying back lost domains and ceding Polish claims to lands held by powerful neighbours in return for peace - he then secured these borders with the construction of a series of castles and the fortification of a number of cities.

During his reign Poland prospered economically: peace encouraged trade and the king grew rich through the raising of taxes. A new silver currency was introduced and, in 1364, Kazimierz passed a law specifically protecting Jews, who formed the bulk of the merchant class, from persecution; thus he was essentially responsible for Poland's great concentration of Jews, which was to disappear during World War II.

In Kraków, trade and industry prospered dramatically and numerous mills, breweries and even a smelting works were constructed. The city saw many brick houses and churches built and the town expanded so fast that within 50 years of being built the city walls had become redundant. It was Kazimierz who founded the city's university as well as three towns around Kraków which have now been incorporated within the city limits: Kazimierz, Kleparz-Florencja and Nowy Okól.

During the fifteenth century, the presence of the royal court, the university and the wealth brought by trade all contributed to Kraków becoming an important centre for humanism (the revival of classical learning with particular emphasis on man's intellectualism, rationality and progress). In 1474 *The Calendar*, the first book published in Poland, was printed here and by the end of the sixteenth century some 70 per cent of the estimated 2500 titles available in Poland had originated in Kraków. Six paper mills operated on the outskirts of the city, such was the demand for paper.

The Renaissance left a massive visual imprint on the city, mainly through royal patronage of Italian artists previously employed in Hungary: Wawel Castle was rebuilt as a Renaissance palace, the cloth halls on Rynek Główny were rebuilt in Renaissance style after a fire in 1555 and the Zygmunt Chapel (in the cathedral) became one of the most important examples of Renaissance architecture north of the Alps.

In 1609 King Zygmunt III left Kraków to march on Russia, which had been threatening Poland's eastern borders. On his return he transferred his court to Warsaw, as it was a more central location for the commonwealth of states, extending to Latvia and Lithuania, to which Poland belonged (and it was also closer to his native Sweden). Though Kraków still remained the place where Poland's kings were crowned and buried, Warsaw subsequently became the centre of Polish political life and hundreds of courtiers, civil servants and hangers on relocated

Boats along the River Wisła are popular in Summer; boats leave from landing stages below Wawel castle

Feeding the pigeons in the Rynek Główny

Above: The tram system in the city is easy and very cheap to use

Right: A quiet moment in the River Wisła

Below: Sightseeing in style, using traditional transport

there, leaving Kraków to fall into a long period of decline.

Invasion and oppression

In the aftermath of the Thirty Years War Sweden became the most powerful military force in Europe. In 1648 the Swedes invaded Poland in what is known as the 'Swedish Deluge'. Kraków was destroyed by the Swedish army in 1655—57, and then again in 1702 during a Polish attempt to seize control of Livonia. The city was rebuilt in grand Baroque style but struggled to regain its former prosperity; the eighteenth century saw repeated devastation by a number of passing foreign armies, the Russians being particularly culpable.

In 1795, following Russian invasion, Poland was partitioned by Austria, Russia and Prussia, and Kraków remained under Austrian rule until 1918 - though at the 1815 Congress of Vienna, in the aftermath of Napoleon's defeat, it was decided that Kraków would become a (theoretically) independent city-state, a status it retained until 1846 when Austria formally re-annexed the city following a local rebellion.

During this period of national oppression Kraków took on a great symbolic importance for the Polish people, with Wawel becoming almost a national shrine. The city once more became a major centre of culture and learning, a number of museums were founded and Lenin even used the city as his base between 1912—4, producing *Pravda* here and directing the international Communist movement.

Poland was finally reconstituted at the end of the First World War and work began to restore Wawel to something like its former glory. Independence was brief, however, and during World War II Kraków (renamed Krakau) became the capital of German-occupied Poland, with Wawel Castle being commandeered by its governor Hans Frank. The most terrible consequence of the German occupation of the city was the loss of almost the entire Jewish community to the nearby death camps. Physically, however, despite the widespread plunder of art treasures, the buildings of Kraków survived the war in pretty good shape - certainly in comparison with the virtual flattening of Warsaw, and indeed most other cities in Poland.

Post-war Communism

After the war, Poland's Communist and Socialist parties united to form the Polish United Workers' Party (PZPR) and, under the auspices of the occupying army of the Soviet Union, a Soviet-style communist system was imposed. Poland became the first line of Soviet defence in the emerging Cold War.

The new regime deemed Kraków's strong cultural, religious and intellectual traditions problematic and so, in an attempt to change its social make-up, built a massive steelworks in the Nowa Huta District, which has unfortunately caused enormous ecological damage to the city, ruining the environment, affecting peoples' health and decaying the city's ancient monuments.

A number of characterless residential areas were built to house the new industrial population (drawn from the surrounding countryside), and these now strangulate the historic centre with typical Eastern European brutality. It's ironic that it was the steelworkers of Nowa Huta, along with the shipyard workers of Gdańsk, who would prove to be the biggest thorn in the side of the Communist regime.

In response to the dire economic crisis of 1980, when the government announced a 100 per cent rise in the price of foodstuffs, a series of strikes took place throughout Poland, most notably at the Gdańsk shipyards where a list of demands, known as the 'Twenty-One Points' were drawn up. As a result of these crippling strikes, in August 1980 the Communist government was forced into conciliation and allowed the formation of a nationwide free trade union, which took the name Solidarity (*Solidarność*). The head of the Gdańsk shipyard workers, Lech Wałęsa, was elected as leader.

The 1980s saw a succession of strikes and factory occupations by Solidarity members, an expression of discontent with the country's chronic economic and social problems. A series of debilitating national strikes in August 1988, combined with the arrival of Gorbachev to power in the Soviet Union, finally led the way to more round table talks in April 1989 where it was agreed that Solidarity could contest a limited number of seats in Poland's forthcoming elections.

Solidarity's overwhelming success in July led the way to the rapid disintegration of communism and in August parliament elected a non-communist prime minister, the journalist Tadeusz Mazowiecki. Acknowledging its inevitable defeat, in January 1990 the Polish United Workers' Party dissolved itself. Later that year, Lech Wałęsa was elected president in the first free elections of the post-Communist era.

With the overthrow of the communist system Kraków is finally addressing its ecological problems (for a brief period the city even had a Green mayor) and regaining its old verve; numerous restaurants, bars, clubs and cinemas have opened and the cultural life of the city has never been more vibrant. In 2004 Poland joined the EU and the huge new shopping complex next to the railway station testifies to the new economic prosperity of the city. In short, Kraków is back on the tourist map with a vengeance, buzzing with visitors, not only from Poland but from all over the world.

Language

Kraków is the most cosmopolitan city in Poland, and as such you can get away with using only the most basic Polish (or even none at all). In tourist circles English is now widely understood (especially amongst the young), however, if you want to get just a little bit more out of your visit it is worth attempting to learn a few key words and phrases.

Unfortunately, with its bewildering array of accents and strings of consonants, Polish is a very daunting language for English speakers. Anybody staying longer than just a few days should consider purchasing a guide book and learning the rules of pronunciation, but, for those who just want a flavour of the language, in the box is a short selection of basic phrases and their phonetic equivalent.

Some Polish Phrases

English	Polish	Pronunciation
Yes	Tak	Tahk
No	Nie	Neh
Please	Proszę	Prosheh
Thank you	Dziękuję	Dzhehnkooyeh
Good morning	Dzień dobry	Dzhehn dobri
Good afternoon	Dzień dobry	Dzhehn dobri
Good evening	Dobry wieczór	Dobri vyehchoor
Goodbye	Do widzenia	Do veedzehnah
Where?	Gdzie?	Gdzheh
When?	Kiedy?	Kyehdi
What?	Co?	Tso
How?	Jak?	Yahk
How much?	Ile?	Eeleh
Who?	Kto?	Kto
Why?	Dlaczego	Dlahechehgo
England	Anglia	Ahnglah
Great Britain	Wielka Brytania	Vyehlkah- Britahyah
I don't understand	Nie rozumiem	Neh-rozoomyehm
Do you speak English?	Czy pan(i)- mówi po- angielsku?	Chi pahn(ee)- moovee po- ahngyehlskoo?
Early/late	Wczesny/późny	Fchehsni/poozni
Cheap/expensive	Tani/drogi	Tahnee/drogee
Near/far	Bliski/daleki	Bleeskee/dahlehkee
Hot/cold	Gorący/zimny	Gorontis/zyeemni
Open/closed	Otwarty/ zamknięty	Offahrti/ zahmknehnti
Old/new	Stary/nowy	Stahri/novi
Beautiful/ugly	Piękny/brzydki	Pyehnkni/bzhitkee
Good/bad	Dobry/zly	Dobri/zwi

1.	Jeden	Yehdehn
2.	Dwa	Dvah
3.	Trzy	Chshi
4.	Cztery	Chtehri
5.	Pięc	Pyehntsh
6.	Sześć	Shehsytsh
7.	Siedem	Syehdehm
8.	Osiem	Osyehm
9.	Dziewięć	Dzhehvyehntsh
10.	Dziesięć	Dzhehsyechnsh

Sunday	Niedziela	Nehdzhehlah
Monday	Poniedzialek	Ponehdz-hahwehk
Tuesday	Wtorek	Ftorehk
Wednesday	Środa	Syrodah
Thursday	Czwartek	Chafartehk
Friday	Piątek	Pyontehk
Saturday	Sobota	Sobotah

Getting around

Some common words you'll see around you.

Polish	**Meaning**
Droga	Road
Główny	Main
Góra	Mountain
Kościól	Church
Miasto	Town
Plac	Square
Rynck	Marketplace
Świety(abbreviated: św)	Saint
Ulica (abbreviated: ul)	Street

Food and Drink

Not only is Kraków the cultural capital of Poland, it is also home to its finest cuisine. Cracovian food, with its goulash, liver sausage and veal cutlets, certainly bears the trace of the city's subjugation under the Austro-Hungarian Empire, though you will detect numerous other influences, notably Russian, Ukrainian and Jewish.

In 1945 the catering trade in Poland was nationalized, and for many years the only places in Kraków where Western visitors could eat out were at the state owned *Orbis* hotel restaurants. However, since the collapse of communism, restaurants, bars, clubs and cafes have appeared at a prodigious rate and by English standards the food is very reasonably priced. A number of restaurants have sprung up offering good-value foreign cuisine: Italian, Oriental, Hungarian, Ukrainian, even Middle-Eastern - check the restaurant index in the Fact File for a selection. Note however that the restaurant trade in the city is very transient with places closing and new ones opening with great frequency.

Traditionally in Poland breakfasts tend to be a spread of eggs, cold meats, jams, cheese and rolls, with a cup of sweet tea or coffee. Poles generally tend to eat their main meal of the day in the late afternoon and then have a light supper (similar to breakfast), though Kraków being such a cosmopolitan place you'll find that the eating habits of the locals match those of most Westerners. If you want a light midday lunch, most of the city's restaurants will serve a snack menu of omelette or sandwiches or salad, or you can visit one of the many Western-style hamburger or pizza joints around the centre (or even the authentically Western McDonalds on Floriańska). Restaurants used to close in the early evening but nowadays, following the dictates of the market, most stay open until midnight. A ten percent tip is the norm.

Most Polish dishes are meat based; chicken (*kurczak*), pork (*wieprzowe*) and beef (*wołowe*) predominate, though the better restaurants will also serve vegetarian dishes (*potrawy jarskie*). Kraków being so tourist orientated, the waiters will generally know enough English to guide you through the menu and assist you in your selection — the menu will usually be multi-lingual anyway (or there will be an English version available). However, be aware that menu prices may be for a particular weight (usually 100g) rather than for the dish itself, and also that you usually pay extra for any accompaniment (salads, potatoes, salads, etc) so that the price on the menu will not necessarily be the price you are charged.

Traditional Polish dishes you will find on the menu include: *barszcz*, a popular beetroot soup sometimes blanched with cream when it becomes *barszcz ukraiński*; *grzybowa*, a delicious wild mushroom soup; *żurek*, rye-flour soup with sour cream; *golonka*, pork knuckle which can be stewed, boiled or roasted and is served with horseradish; *kiszka*, black pudding; *bigos*, a meat and cabbage stew; *pieczeń z dzika*, roasted wild boar; *pstràg z grilla*, which is grilled trout; *pierogi*, dumplings stuffed with cheese, minced meat, cabbage and/or mushrooms; *zraz zawijany*, stewed beef in a sour cream sauce; *gołàbki*, cabbage

A beer, a map and a guidebook... planning the day's sightseeing at an open-air cafe

leaves stuffed with rice and minced beef and sometimes mushrooms; *flaczki*, which is tripe.

One delicacy you will undoubtedly come across when walking around the old town is *oscypki*, an unpasteurised smoked sheep's cheese, which is made in the highlands by the locals to secret recipies and sold from baskets on street corners by old women (though a good shop to look for it in is Pod Aniołami at Grodzka 35). The cheese will be in small spindle-shaped forms, often with a decorative pattern imprinted on it. Production of this cheese dates at least as far back as medieval times.

As an accompaniment to your meal, there are the usual variety of mineral waters, soft drinks and coffees you would expect back home. Tea (*herbata*) is traditionally served in a glass and without milk (Poles tend to like it heavily-sugared) while coffee (*kawa*) is traditionally very black and very bitter - though most places now will give you the typical selection of Western style

Vodka

Vodka comes in a bewildering variety of colourings and flavourings, examples include: Zubrówka, imbued with the scent of bison grass, the stem of which is usually left in the bottle; Pieprzówka, a peppered variety, which is a well-renowned cold-remedy; Wiśniówka boasts a pleasant cherry flavour, while Ctrynówka is lemon-tinged; harder to find is Miodowka, which is honeyed; Pajsachówka is recommended for hardened drinkers only, as it is 75 per cent proof. As far as clear vodkas go, Cracovia enjoys a particularly good reputation. Clear vodka is usually served neat and cold and with a separate glass of water, the flavoured varieties are taken warm. You down it in one with the traditional toast of "Na zdrowie" (cheers).

cappuccinos and espressos. Beer (*piwo*) connoisseurs will want to look out for the local brands 'Żywiec' and 'Okocim', which go down quite smoothly, though Western beers are generally available at more inflated prices (though they're still cheaper than back home, as the increasing number of British 'tourists' attracted to the city for a Friday night out regrettably testifies). Most of the wines available will be from Hungary or Bulgaria - again, Western wines will be more expensive. If you're feeling like getting really into the spirit of things then ask for vodka (*wódka*), which is a Polish institution in itself, though the general orientation in the bars around the centre is towards beer, particularly amongst the young.

Alternative spirits are the delicious plum brandy *śliwowica* or its more aggressive cousin *winiak*, a throat-scarring grape brandy readily available in most restaurants and cafes. You might also like to try out the mead (*miód pitny*) that is increasingly available. Mead is often called a "honey wine" (and some unscupulous types have advertised white wine with honey added as mead), but it is in fact a distinct alcoholic beverage made of honey, water and yeast - and often containing herbs and spices and even fruit. Traditionally it was made in Europe (often by monks) in places where grapes could not grow, and there many different varieties available; in Poland the different types of mead are categorised according to the ratio of honey to water used, so you get *półtorak* (2:1), *dwójniak* (1:1), *trójniak* (1:2) and *czwórniak* (1:3). A very fine sweet mead available, often served as a dessert, is 'Jadwiga Mead' which is made with a 3:1 ratio (and classified as a *półtorak*).

Climate

Kraków has a continental climate pattern, with summers occasionally uncomfortably hot, and winters usually

Min and max temps in °C (and °F)

Jan	-5/0	(23/32)
Feb	-5/1	(23/34)
March	-1/7	(30/45)
April	3/13	(37/55)
May	9/20	(48/68)
June	12/24	(54/75)
July	14/24	(57/75)
Aug	13/24	(55/75)
Sept	8/19	(46/66)
Oct	4/13	(39/55)
Nov	0/7	(32/45)
Dec	-3/3	(27/37)

Rainfall in mm (and inches)

Jan	26	(1)
Feb	26	(1)
March	37	(1.5)
April	44	(1.75)
May	48	(2)
June	92	(3.75)
July	113	(4.5)
Aug	89	(3.5)
Sept	64	(2.5)
Oct	51	(2)
Nov	39	(1.5)
Dec	34	(1.25)

Above Left: Paintings for sale on the streets of Kraków
Above Right: Kraków is a city of music
Below: Outside the Isaac Synagogue

very cold. Autumn and spring are the most pleasant times to visit. Rain falls frequently in spring, summer and autumn – in summer often in short, sharp thunderstorms in late afternoon or early evening, making it the wettest time of the year. Snow is usual in winter, and from December to February the roads undergo regular clearing with snowploughs and dumper trucks.

When to visit

Kraków is one of the premier tourist destinations in central Europe and in summer it can get very crowded. This, coupled with the sometimes unpleasantly hot weather, means that the best times to visit are probably early or late summer – or, even better, spring or autumn. A visit in winter (any time from November to March) needs careful consideration. On the down side, it can be bitterly, unpleasantly cold, with an endless succession of gloomy, snowy days; some tourist attractions close and most curtail their opening times. On the plus side, the city can look fantastic on a snowy day when the sun shines, there are far fewer tourists around, and many hotels slash their rates during this time. Christmas is a very special and atmospheric time to be in the city (see p.31).

A list of annual cultural and religious events is given on p.135. This might also influence your choice of which time of year to visit. The cultural scene is busy all year round but major festivals seem to congregate in spring, summer and early Autumn, with January and February comparatively quiet months on the cultural scene.

Further Reading

The standard history of Poland is Norman Davies' two-part *God's Playground*, though its size hardly makes it holiday reading so alternatively you could try his one-stop shop *Heart of Europe: The Past in Poland's Present.* Countless books have been written on the Holocaust, if you want a thorough overview then you should go for Martin Gilbert's *The Holocaust*, or for something a little more digestible *Auschwitz, the Nazis and the Final Solution* by Laurence Rees. However, for history to really come alive it's often best to head for personal memoirs; *The Kraków Ghetto Pharmacy*, written by the only non-Jewish inhabitant of the Kraków Ghetto Tadeusz Pankiewicz, and *Commandant of Auschwitz*, written by Rudolf Hoess in Kraków in the days before his execution, provide two powerful yet very different ways in to the subject - both have been recently reprinted. Thomas Keneally's Booker Prize-winning *Schindler's Ark*, which tells the story of how industrialist Oscar Schindler saved the lives of 1100 Jews by providing them with work in his factory, is also well worth seeking out - especially if you've seen the film *Schindler's List.*

For personal reflections on the great social and political forces that affected Poland during the twentieth century two works by Czesław Miłosz stand out - *The Captive Mind* and *Native Realm*; the former is a psychological study of those writers and intellectuals who had found accommodation with the communist regime, while the latter is a relaxed autobiography of sorts relecting on the great wash of history as directly experienced by him up until his defection to the West.

In terms of fiction, probably Poland's most internationally-renowned writer is Stanisław Lem (see box) whose remorselessly intelligent works are particularly recommended for those who prefer science fiction to fantasy. *Solaris* is his most famous novel, and it's a work that focuses not so much on the unknown as the foibles and frailties of the main characters - a mission is undertaken to study a strange planet covered by a huge ocean whose precise makeup no-one can determine, but in the end the universe, as usual, gives no easy answers and the astronauts are left questioning only themselves. For an evocation of Jewish life in pre-war Poland try seeking out the novels of Isaac Bashevis Singer - *The Family Moskat* is set in Warsaw but is a good choice. Anyone looking for something a little more avant garde might want to give the intellectually playful and bizarrely humourous works of Witold Gombrowicz a go - *Ferdydurke* and *Pornografia* (which isn't pornographic) are the most well-known. Arguably the most famous work of fiction written by a Pole is *Quo Vadis?* which earned Henryk Sienkiewicz the Nobel Prize; this is an epic blockbuster which tells

Wisława Szymborska

Poet and Kraków resident Wisława Szymborska was the surprise winner of the Nobel Prize for literature in 1996. Though little known outside her country's borders at the time of the award, a selection of Szymborska's work is now available in English under the title *View with a Grain of Sand* and it's well worth seeking out. Born in 1923 in the town of Kórnik in Western Poland, Szymborska has lived in Kraków since 1931. A skilled translator as well as poet, she has published only a dozen or so volumes of poetry but her simplicity of thought and mastery of technique have combined to produce some truly memorable verse.

Stanisław Lem

Stanisław Lem was a prolific writer of novels, short stories, literary criticism and philosophy, though it is as a science fiction writer that he is best known. Born in Lwów in 1921, Lem originally studied medicine, though he declined to take his final exams in order to avoid a career as a military doctor. He moved to Kraków in 1946 when Poland's borders were redrawn and Lwów found itself in the Soviet Union. Lem published his first science fiction work in 1951 and in 1961 he wrote what has become his most enduring work *Solaris* (which has been twice filmed). *Solaris* was Lem's first book to be published in America; his work has since been translated into thirty-six languages and has sold an estimated twenty million copies worldwide. In 1982, after martial law was imposed, Lem left Poland to live in Vienna, though he returned to his homeland in 1988 to live in Kraków. He died in 2006.

the story of the early Christians in Rome, and is said to be an allegory of the Polish struggles during the partition of the country. Connoisseurs of the classics might fancy taking on Jan Potocki's *Tales from the Saragossa Manuscript: Ten days in the life of Alphonse von Worden*, which is a very long novel written in French by a Pole and set in Spain; it tells a number of inter-related tales in a variety of different styles, resembling something along the lines of *The Arabian Nights*.

The Trumpeter of Kraków by Eric P.Kelly is a children's book, aimed at children of around 11/12, which tells of a boy who, with his parents, comes to Kraków in 1461 as a refugee from the Tartar incursions into the Ukraine; the real "star" of the book, though, is medieval Kraków itself, in all its glory – featuring alchemists, students at the Jagiellonian University, the *Hejnał* trumpeter (see p.35) and an appearance by King Kazimierz IV Jagiellończyk himself.

If epic poetry is your thing then you might want to try Adam Mickiewicz's *Pan Tadeusz*, a tale of life in rural Lithuania in the early nineteenth century, which has become a Polish classic (even though Lithianians and Belarussians as well as Poles claim Mickiewicz as their own). For more bite-sized offerings, the works of Czesław Miłosz (see box p.85) and Kraków resident and Nobel Prize winner Wisława Szymborska are highly recommended and widely available in English translation. *The Burning Forest*, edited by Adam Czerniawski, is a pretty good anthology of Polish verse. In terms of drama, Stanisław Wyspiańki's *The Wedding* is available in an English version by Noel Clark (which matches the original's rhyming poetry), but works by Tadeusz Kantor are very hard to get hold of; *Wielopole/Wielopole* was last published back in 1990, or you could try looking for *A Journey Through Other Spaces*, a collection of insightful essays by Kantor together with a critical study of his work by Michal Kobialka.

Film-lovers will want to get a hold of Andrzej Wajda's short but interesting *Double Vision: My Life in Film*. *Roman by Polański* has been out of print a long time but it is worth trying to get hold of a copy; the book contains an interesting section on life in the Podgórze Ghetto. *Kieślowski on Kieślowski* is the best book available on the man who, by virtue of the *Three Colours Trilogy*, has been Poland's most internationally-acclaimed film-maker of recent years.

Food-enthusiasts might want to check out an excellent piece of recipie and historical food writing called *Old Polish Traditions: In the Kitchen and at the Table* by Mary Lemnis and Henryk Vitry. Other good options available include *The Best of Polish Cooking* by Karen West and *The Polish Kitchen* by Mary Pinińska.

Above: The Cathedral Museum
Below Left: The Towers of St Mary's Church

Places to Visit

1. Central Kraków

Rynek Główny and St Mary's Church (page 27 and 34)

The principal church of the Old Town sits on the corner of the Rynek Główny, the main square, one of the most beautiful and expansive urban spaces in Europe.

Czartoryski Museum (page 40)

Poland's greatest art gallery and historical museum. Exhibits include everything from paintings by Leonardo and Rembrandt to Egyptian mummies.

Floriańska Street (page 36)

The principal shopping street in the city, a pedestrianised avenue running north from the Rynek Główny lined with elegant boutiques and expensive hotels.

2. Wawel Castle and the Cathedral

The Cathedral (page 60)

A shrine to Polish nationhood, the Cathedral was built in the fourteenth century in Gothic style. Its hilltop location has meant that, rather than extending or enlarging, it has undergone numerous architectural refurbishments – most obviously in its chapels which present a cross-section of architectural styles through the centuries.

The Royal Chambers (page 68)

The bareness of the castle interior sums up its sad history of plunder over the centuries, but the magnificence of the friezes and hanging tapestries reflect something of the old opulence.

3. Kazimierz

Old Synagogue (page 77)

The oldest surviving synagogue in Poland. It ceased to function after being destroyed by the Nazis and now houses a museum commemorating Jewish culture.

Rumuh Synagogue and Cemetery (page 78)

An intimate structure dating from the sixteenth century, backed by an evocative cemetery, containing valuable Renaissance-style tombstones.

The Church on the Rock (page 84)

A keystone of Polish history, as it is the place where St Stanisław, the patron saint of Poland, was martyred.

4. Excursions

Wieliczka Salt Mine (page 96)

An amazing and unmissable excursion from the city centre; miles of underground passages featuring odd rock formations, underground lakes and even a chapel carved completely out of the salt. On the UNESCO World Cultural Heritage List, it has been in operation for 700 years.

5. Auschwitz-Birkenau

An unforgettable and harrowing encounter.

Paintings for sale outside the Sukiennice (the medieval Cloth Hall)

1. The Old Town

This walk around Kraków's Old Town *(Stare Miasto)*, including a good look round all the museums, might take a whole day with a stop for lunch; those who like to linger in the many shops, churches and museums covered by the tour will easily take two days to see everything. The tour starts in the **Rynek Główny**, the main square, where you'll find the city's most famous church, **St Mary's**; after that it takes you along Floriańska, the main shopping street, to the **Czartoryski Museum**, home to the finest art and historical collections in the city.

Opposite & Left: The Rynek Główny is lined with open-air cafes and restaurants

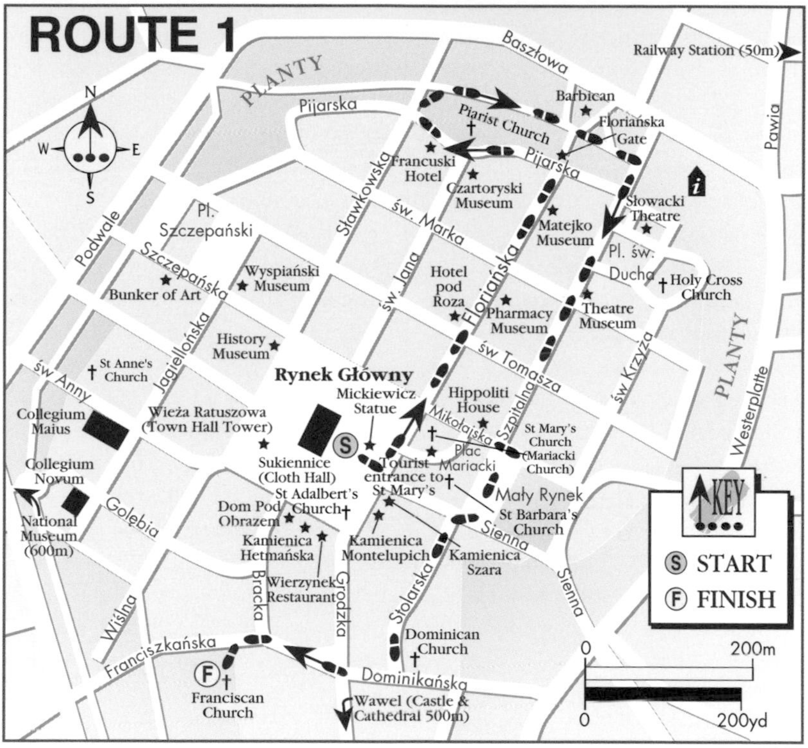

The route then runs through part of the **Planty**, the attractive area of greenery that circles the city, and across the peaceful square **Mały Rynek**, before ending up at the **Dominican and Franciscan churches**.

Separate features in this chapter look at further **art galleries**, and also the **Jagiellonian University**, the oldest in Poland, the historic heart of which lies to the west of the Rynek.

Rynek Główny

The **Rynek Główny** – literally the 'Main Market-place' – is one of the most expansive and attractive city squares in Europe. It is the focal point of the city, a grand and historic plaza that hums with energy and exerts an almost magnetic pull for both tourists and residents. You will find yourself returning time and time again to enjoy the sumptuous collection of ancient buildings, the wide traffic-free open spaces, the shops and restaurants and bars, and the street musician and jugglers; one of the chief delights of Kraków is simply to spend time people-watching in the open-air cafes (if it's warm enough to sit outside) or to browse for books or souvenirs in the shops that line the square. Laid out from scratch in 1257 after Tartar invasions had devastated the old city, and specifically mentioned in the royal charter from that year drawn up by Duke Bolesław the Chaste, the square has been the liveliest part of central Kraków for over seven hundred years. In the summer street musicians, flower-sellers, horse-drawn carriages and tour groups mingle here from dusk until late into the night. During the winter the square is the main focus of a Cracovian Christmas, with a hot red wine called *grzaniec* from the Galicia region of Poland sold at stalls set up in the shadow of a magnificently decorated Christmas tree whose base is strewn with oversized "presents"; at this time of year you will also be able to buy delicacies from stallholders such as almonds, roasted nuts, and dried fruits covered in chocolate.

The square is divided into two halves (east and west) by the **Sukiennice** (see p.30), formerly the medieval cloth hall, now occupied by shops downstairs and an art gallery upstairs. Most of the buildings lining the square are neo-classical, often with medieval cellars. The **Wieża Ratuszowa** in the south-west corner of the square is the medieval tower of the former town hall, the rest of which was pulled down in 1820 owing to general dilapidation. The former building, dating from around 1300, also contained a prison, a storage place for merchants' goods, and a torture chamber. Two lions now guard the entrance to the tower (there is a legend that if a virtuous maiden sits on the back of one of them they will roar), and just inside the main door are various photographic and historical exhibitions. Predictably it's the view from the top, over the rooftops and spires of Kraków, which is the tower's biggest attraction (unfortunately it is open rather erratic hours and is often closed in the winter). A café has been set up in the old cellars of the building (entrance from the opposite side).

In the south-eastern corner of the Rynek Główny is a tiny church, **St Adalbert's**, whose interior is intimate and dark, and also rather plain. It's one of the oldest churches in the city, founded at least a thousand years ago on a spot where St Adalbert preached in 997 before setting off to convert the Prussians. The age of the church is the reason why it stands out of alignment with the rest of the streets and sides of the square; it was here long before they were laid out. Although there's a Romanesque flavour to the building, what you see now dates mainly from the eighteenth century. In the crypt (unfortunately closed much of the time) is a small exhibition on the history of the Rynek, and you can also see original medieval water pipes and a twelfth century skeleton.

Close by is a statue (1898) of the Polish dramatist and poet **Adam Mickiewicz**. Mickiewicz was born in Lithuania (then part of Poland) in 1798 and studied at Vilnius University, where he was arrested for spreading Polish nationalism and deported to Russia. He spent much of his adult life there and in France and Italy. He died in Istanbul in 1855, whilst on a mission to quell arguments that had broken out in Polish forces preparing to fight against Russia in the Crimea, and is buried in Wawel

Buildings Lining the Rynek Główny

In medieval times the level of the Rynek was about half a storey lower than it is at present; what are now the cellars of the Town Hall were originally the building's ground floor, while the original Romanesque portal of St Adalbert's Church is a full two metres below the current level of the square. However, successive paving projects raised the level of the square – and dried it out, too (in medieval times the whole expanse was often a muddy quagmire). Meanwhile as the centuries progressed the medieval houses surrounding the square were gradually rebuilt (after many were destroyed in fires) in the Renaissance and later styles. Most are the former houses of rich merchants, and many of them are now interesting buildings in their own right. Number six, situated opposite the Mickiewicz statue, is known as the "Grey House" (the **Kamienica Szara**); the building dates back to the thirteenth century, and its more recent façade hides some remaining Gothic rooms in the interior. The celebrated rebel leader Tadeusz Kościuszko used the building as a Headquarters during the 1794 uprising against the Russian invasion of Poland (see p.97). Its ground floor now houses a smart restaurant. Next door at number 7, the **Kamienica Montelupich** (also known as *Dom Włoski* – the Italian House) was once the home of the Montelupi family, a dynasty of Italian merchants who made their fortune in Kraków. The building has a distinctive Renaissance entrance and once housed Poland's first Post Office. On the south side of the square, another mansion houses the **Wierzynek Restaurant**, which claims to be the oldest restaurant in the city, its royal charter dating back to 1364. It is said that in that year a wealthy merchant, Mikołaj Wierzynek, honoured King Kazimierz the Great with a feast at this spot; the guest list included the Holy Roman Emperor Charles IV and King Lajos of Hungary. More recently, Presidents George Bush (senior), Nixon, Mitterrand and de Gaulle have all eaten at the restaurant commemorating the host of that original royal feast. Next door to the right the Baroque portal of the **Kamienica Hetmańska** gives access to shops whose the Gothic vaults are still surviving, and two doors further along is the **Dom Pod Obrazem**, formerly the house of a wealthy family of burghers. Its exterior wall is decorated with a striking picture of the Madonna painted in 1718.

cathedral. Many of his dramatic works were premiered in Kraków; his poem *Pan Tadeusz* (written in Paris in 1834 and made into a film by leading Polish director Andrzej Wajda in 1999) is considered to be something of a national epic, even though its opening lines are *Lithuania, My Homeland* (Lithuania was part of Poland at the time). The allegorical figures surrounding the statue are, facing the cloth hall, a bare-chested warrior with shield and sword, representing patriotism; education is represented by a man tutoring a young boy, whose hand rests expectantly on a thick book, while on the other side of the statue, the "echo" of this image is a woman and a young girl, representing poetry; finally, the maiden facing Sienna Street represents the motherland. The statue courted controversy when it was built – Jan Matejko, the city's most famous artist, lost out in a competition to design it to Teodor Rygier, who was forced to replace some of the figures shortly after its unveiling as some

The Sukiennice

Over 100 metres (300 yards) long and more or less slicing the square in two is the medieval clothhall known as the **Sukiennice**. Once the centre of the town's textile and clothing market, it's tourists rather than textile merchants who make up the buyers here nowadays. Created initially in connection with a trading charter granted to the town in 1306, the first building on this site was constructed between 1344 and 1392 to replace the market stalls that once stood here. Following a fire, the Sukiennice was extensively renovated (and prettified) in the 1550s (when the undulating façade with its gargoyles was built by a Florentine stonemason, Santi Gucci) and then again in 1875 (when the Venetian-style arcades on each side, and the coats of arms of Polish cities you can see at both ends, were added). Besides being busy with shoppers, the building is also the grand setting for important civic functions.

The **central gallery**, as dark and busy as a Middle Eastern bazaar, is lined with stalls where you can buy chess sets, inlaid ornaments, walking sticks, jewellery and dolls. Some of what's on offer has a connection with the city but much of it doesn't. Here for example you can buy a "cK: city of Kraków" T-shirt, with a logo on the front parodying the famous Calvin Klein design; the old medieval cloth traders are probably revolving in their graves at the thought of it all. However, amongst all the tourist tat there are some genuine craft items on offer, such as amber jewellery and thick woollen jumpers from Podhale, the mountainous region south of Kraków. Outside, the **arcades** accessible from the square house a number of cafes, the most famous of which is the **Noworolski**, across from St Adalbert's Church (p.147).

Upstairs (the entrance is in the central part of the east-facing side of the building) is the **Gallery of Nineteenth Century Polish Art**. Heroic battles and idyllic pastoral scenes form the basis of the collection, and the most striking feature of many paintings is their breathtaking size (some taking up whole walls) and attention to detail. The principal painter represented here is Jan Matejko (1838 – 1893, see p.38), associated all his life with the city of Kraków, whose lush, romantic depiction of triumphal scenes from Polish history have made him famous in this country. One of his paintings is *Homage of Prussia (Hołd Pruski)*, which depicts Albrecht of Hohenzollern, the leader of the Teutonic Order of Knights, kneeling before the King of Poland on the Rynek Główny; this event took place on 10th April 1525 and marked the end of the Knights' independent state. Other famous paintings here are *Four in Hand* by Józef Chełmoński (1881), which shows a team of horses tearing across the plains with such authenticity that the viewer almost feels the need to jump out of their way; *The Blue Hussars* by Piotr Michałowski, a romantic image of soldiers on horseback painted against a creamy, deep-yellow sky; and *Szal Uniesien (Blissful Frenzy)* by Władisław Podkowiński (1894), which features a naked red-haired maiden clutching hold of the neck of a raging black stallion – a frenzied, arresting and memorable example of the symbolist style. (Supposedly the figure in the painting was the wife of one of the Podkowiński's friends and the object of his unrequited passion – which might account for the fact that the painter himself once tried to damage the painting with a knife when it was hanging in the gallery; evidence of the cuts can still be seen, despite restoration work.)

Town Hall Tower (left) and Sukiennice (right)

Kraków at Christmas – the *szopki*

If you're in Kraków during the weeks either side of Christmas you'll see a lot of *szopki*. They're essentially hand-made cribs representing the nativity scene, built of wood, cardboard, silver foil and the like, crammed with detail and bright colours and usually based around a representation of a church (which often looks suspiciously like St Mary's). Cribs vary in size from fussily-decorated miniatures you can hold in your hand to models that need to be taken round in a truck; they normally come complete with tiny moveable figures and multi-coloured fairy lights. Figures in the scenes, besides Mary and Joseph, can include characters from local legends, Polish folklore, and even politicians or local celebrities.

The tradition of their manufacture dates back to the days of St Francis of Assisi in thirteenth century Italy, who thought that the cribs might be a good way of bringing the events of the Christmas story to the illiterate masses. His ideas were taken up by a number of religious orders, including the Jesuits, who spread the tradition to Austria, and the Franciscans, who brought them to Kraków. In fact the tradition of making cribs can be seen in many parts of central Europe, although the Kraków cribs are unusual in their prominent use of a local church (rather than a stable) as the setting. In the eighteenth and nineteenth centuries, the cribs became a backdrop for folk puppet shows known as *jasełki*, with the figures being made to move by puppeteers. Often the puppet shows were pieces of political satire that mocked the ruling Austro-Hungarian empire, while the story of the nativity somewhat faded into the background.

Nowadays, thanks to an enterprising art historian named Jerzy Dobrzycki, there is a competition each year to find the best crib. The first competition was held in 1937; the organizers are the Kraków Historical Museum, of which Dobrzycki was curator. The competition is held the first Thursday of December, when the competing cribs are displayed in the morning around the Mickiewicz statue. Winning models are then exhibited in the Kraków Historical Museum, usually until the beginning of February, and you may be able to see the year's winning crib displayed year-round in the museum's front window. Both the Kraków Historical Museum, and the Ethnographic Museum, display *szopki* from previous years, and you can often find mass-produced *szopki* for sale in souvenir shops.

The Veit Stoss Grand Altar

This is easily the most famous feature of St Mary's Church and is what most people come to the church to see. The incredible altar was sculpted by a German, Veit Stoss (known to Poles as Wit Stwosz), who was born in Horb am Neckar in the Black Forest in around 1438 and came to Kraków from Nuremberg in 1477. He was probably invited to the city by the community of German merchants who lived here, and who worshipped in the Mariacki church, although his somewhat combative manner might have led to a falling-out with the Nuremberg authorities which provided another reason for him to come here. Stoss spent twenty years of his life in Kraków, exempted from paying taxes by the city elders while he worked on his first major commission, which was to become one of the finest pieces of late Gothic art in Europe.

Stoss actually supervised the building of the altar out in the ulica Grodzka, where students and carvers fashioned it over the course of twelve years in full view of the city burghers, who spent the equivalent of the town's annual budget on their ostentatious commission. The design is framed by oakwood but the sculptures are fashioned from the wood of the plane tree, which traditionally is associated with the Virgin Mary. The altar was unveiled and consecrated on July 25th 1489. Originally it was intended that it be opened only on major religious festivals; nowadays it's opened every day (excluding Sundays and Saints' Days) at 11.50am.

When closed, the altar's twelve pictorial panels include representations of the birth of the Virgin Mary (middle left), the presentation of the infant Christ in the Temple (bottom row, second from left) and, to the right of this, the placing of Christ's body in the tomb and then the risen Christ appearing to Mary Magdalene (bottom right panel). The top row depicts the Capture of Christ (second from left); to the right of this is the Crucifixion, and below this the Lamentation (lowering of Christ from the Cross), a scene influenced by Dutch painting styles.

When the shutters open, the central design consisting of 200 sculpted

people didn't like them. During the Second World War the Nazis dismantled the statue, intending to sell the metal for scrap, but the various parts were found intact in Hamburg after the war, allowing the structure to be reconstructed. Nowadays it is something of a city centre gathering and meeting place, and just north of it are traditional haunts of flower-sellers and pigeon-feeders.

At the square's northwestern corner, the Krzysztofory Palace (named after St Christopher), a seventeenth century mansion created by joining a number of burghers' houses together, is now the **Kraków History Museum**. Not surprisingly the exhibits here relate to the historical development of the city, figures is revealed. The figures are anything between three centimetres and three metres high, and all have a part to play in a depiction of the Dormition (i.e. final sleep) of the Virgin Mary. Actually, the Virgin Mary appears three times – in the centre of the panel, where she is raised to heaven by eight angels, along with Christ (the Assumption); in the lower part, where St John waits to cover her with a cape as she enters her "final sleep"; and at the top where she is crowned, flanked by St Stanislaw and St Adalbert (this last part of the sculpture is also visible when the shutters are closed). The Apostles who surround Mary in the central part of the scene are actually slightly larger than life size and were supposedly modelled by contemporary Cracovians. The six pictorial representations on the wings of the opened altar, either side of the central scene, are on the left the Annunciation (appearance of the Angel Gabriel to Mary), the birth of Christ, and the visit of the three Kings; and on the right the Resurrection, the ascent of Christ into heaven, and the events of Pentecost. Throughout the design, the mastery of detail, the drama conveyed by the use of three different depths of relief, and the theological complexity of the scenes portrayed all lend weight to the off-used tag of "masterpiece" actually being appropriate in this instance; Pablo Picasso, who saw the altar in 1948, is reported to have called it the "eighth wonder of the world".

Following the creation of this altarpiece, and the fashioning of tombs in Wawel Cathedral and the Dominican Church, Veit Stoss returned to Nuremberg in 1496. There he became out of step with the new styles of the Italian renaissance and Protestant reformation, both of which took hold in Nuremberg and became important influences on artistic style there. His most famous work in Nuremberg is the Annunciation, a sculpture suspended from the ceiling of the city's Church of St Lorenz. Other than that, however, Stoss mainly produced comparatively unremarkable wooden statues, a far cry from the glorious work he made in Kraków. Later in his lift he got into debt and forged a document, for which he was branded on both cheeks and forbidden from travelling beyond Nuremberg, where he died in 1533.

and include armoury, epic paintings showing scenes from Kraków's tumultuous history, plus civic documents, shields and charters from medieval times to the twentieth century. There's a good amount of information in English, and ancient Kraków is brought to life particularly well through films and models showing the city in centuries gone by. But the *szopki* (nativity scenes) are the most obvious draw, particularly during December and January when they are all displayed downstairs and make a visit to the museum during those months a real delight; at other times of year you might need to ask the curators to show you some examples as the cribs are not always on display.

St Mary's Church

The most noteworthy feature of the Rynek Główny is **St Mary's Church** *(Kościół Mariacki*, the Church of Our Lady or the Mariacki Church) in the north-eastern corner. The principal house of Christian worship in Kraków's old town, the church is always bustling with the pious and the curious, and with priests hearing confession as nuns scuttle by; services take place more or less constantly throughout the day, and worshippers of course have priority over tourists when it comes to visiting. In the evenings the Mariacki is also a venue for organ recitals and other concerts.

The present building was founded in 1290 on the site of at least two previous churches, and was funded as a 'people's church' by rich city merchants who deliberately set out to create a church that would rival the royal pomp of Wawel Cathedral. What you see today is a Gothic brick construction built between 1355 and 1395, a triple-aisled basilica with side chapels added in the fifteenth century and an effusive baroque interior dating from the eighteenth.

The main entrance to the church is on the Rynek Główny. This ornate late Baroque porch dates from 1752 and is usually reserved for worshippers. Tourists must enter the building through an entrance on the south side which opens onto a small square, **Plac Mariacki**. Until 1796 this space formed the cemetery of the church (the small church on the other side of the square, **St Barbara's**, served as the cemetery church, and according to legend was built from bricks left over after the construction of St Mary's). The different coloured paving stones on the Plac Mariacki indicate the positions of the former gates and walls of the cemetery, while the exterior walls of both churches are marked with funerary inscriptions. Most of those buried here were rich city merchants and burghers. For a time many of the richest merchants were German speakers, and the sermons were delivered in St Mary's in German; those who wanted to listen to a sermon in Polish had to go to St Barbara's. By one of the doors on the south side of St Mary's are some iron shackles, use to restrain medieval lawbreakers, while the statue in the square

Rynek Główny, the city's main square, is one of the most attractive urban spaces in Europe

is a 1958 copy of one of the figures on Veit Stoss's famous altar, which is the focal point of the church itself.

Much of the church interior is off-limits to tourists. You probably won't be able to see the copy of the **Black Madonna of Częstochowa** (see p.109) which is ornamented by a Papal crown bestowed by Cardinal Stefan Wyszynski in 1968. However, you will be able to appreciate the slender, elegant proportions of the church, and

The Legend of the Two Towers

The most obvious feature of the facade of St Mary's Church is that the two towers, both dating from the fifteenth century, are of different heights and styles. As you face the church from the Rynek, the left-hand (taller) tower, 81m high, is topped with an eight-sided upper storey and a spire (dating from 1478) while the right-hand tower, shorter by some twelve metres, is topped by a crown that dates from 1548. A Kraków legend has it that the architects who built the towers were brothers. The elder brother, full of confidence, built the left-hand tower without proper preparation and had to shorten the length of each storey to make the structure stable. His younger brother built more slowly but his tower had better foundations and his elder brother realized that this tower would eventually be architecturally superior to his own. In a fit of jealousy, the elder brother killed his sibling with an iron knife and then threw himself off his tower; the murder weapon still hangs from a chain at the entrance to the Sukiennice. (In reality, the two towers were originally built to the same height and then one of them had extra storeys added later; the iron knife hanging in the Sukiennice was simply a reminder to the townsfolk of Kraków of the swiftness of medieval judgment.)

The bugle call – the *hejnał Mariacki* – which sounds from the taller of the two towers of St Mary's will be a familiar feature of Kraków after you've been in the city a couple of days. It is played every hour by a trumpeter, and at night, when all is quiet in the city, you can hear it from most parts of the old town. Except during the Nazi occupation a version of the tune has been played every hour, every day, since 1810, and since 1927 the noonday call has been broadcast by Polish state radio.

Something of a symbol of national pride and defiance, the tradition of the bugle call is centuries old, although it has fallen into abeyance for long periods (sometimes due to the absence of a trumpeter). Famously the melody ends abruptly, in mid-phrase (rather like the *Last Post*). It recalls a legend that an earlier trumpeter was killed by an arrow in his throat in 1241 when his call warned of an approaching Tartar invasion. However, *Hejnał* means "dawn" in Hungarian and it is more likely that the tradition of the call dates from the days of King Louis the Hungarian in the fourteenth century, when the bugle call was sounded in the morning as a signal to open the gates of the city. The hourly playing of the call probably dates from the seventeenth century, and the actual tune currently played was composed by an American, Eric Kelly, who taught American studies in the Jagiellonian University in the 1920s and is the author of a children's book entitled The *Trumpeter of Kraków* (see p.22).

the rich friezes on the walls, painted by Jan Matejko, whose paintings you might have seen in the Sukiennice art gallery (see p.30). His awesomely beautiful **ceiling** (dating from the 1890s) consists of a myriad of stars painted on a blue background; he also designed the tracery of the Great West window. The stone **Crucifix** at the entrance to the Choir was designed, like the altar, by Veit Stoss and is an exquisitely moving work, featuring the crucified Christ set against a background of the Old City of Jerusalem. Next to it, the sixteenth century, four-sided alabaster **ciborium** acts as a receptacle for the Eucharist.

You'll possibly have to pay to see the church's most famous feature, the **Veit Stoss Grand Altar** in the chancel (see p.32). Be there in the morning (daily except Sundays and Saints Days) at around 11.45am to see the altar unveiled in a slightly surreal ceremony. To the accompaniment of rousing orchestral music delivered from the specially-installed sound system, the altarpiece is opened up by a nun, and the polyglot tourist guides begin their spiel after the final rousing chords have died away.

This is the only occasion when you get to see the altar, which remains closed up at other times. After it's been shown, most visitors head back into the square to hear the noon trumpet call from the church tower, which always brings a round of applause.

The Enchanted Knights

According to legend, the pigeons in the Rynek Główny, which cluster around the entrance to St Mary's Church, are actually the enchanted knights in the service of a thirteenth century Duke, Henryk Probus. He wanted to be crowned King of Poland but needed the money for the journey to Rome to receive papal blessing for his coronation. He made a pact with a witch that she would lend him some money, provided that he left some of his knights behind as security for the loan. The witch then duly turned the knights into pigeons. Unfortunately, the duke gambled and drank away all his money, and returned from his journey without his promised crown; with the loan unpaid, the witch refused to turn the pigeons back into knights, and to this day they remain fluttering around in the square.

Along Floriańska

From St Mary's, the crowds drift up **ulica Floriańska**, the busiest shopping street in the city. Here you will find private travel agents, expensive hotels such as the Pod Różą (see p.39), chic clothing and jewellery stores and a not-so-chic McDonald's outlet (at the far end).

It's an ancient thoroughfare, laid out and named in the thirteenth century as part of the so-called 'Royal Way', the processional route which Polish monarchs took on their route to Wawel. Many of the buildings are distinctive and garnished with various designs and ornaments. For instance at No 5 there is a niche with a stone renaissance figure of the Virgin and Child (marooned somewhat above a rather ordinary kebab shop), and outside no.17 (opposite the Pod Różą Hotel) there

The Hipoliti House

Behind the rear of St Mary's church, on Mikołajska, the Hipoliti House (Kamenica Hipolitów), named after a family of Italian cloth merchants that once owned this medieval townhouse, is a museum in which different styles of domestic interiors through the ages have been faithfully reconstructed. Some of the rooms still have their original eighteenth century stuccoed ceilings, which were grafted on to a dwelling whose origins date back to the fourteenth century. From the ground floor entrance, with its sixteenth century vaulting, steep steps lead up to the first floor, where an eighteenth century bedroom boasts exuberant Rococo furniture, a Venetian mirror and a table clock manufactured by Gotfryd Krosz, watchmaker to the King of Poland, whose workshop was in Kraków. Another room on this floor is a nineteenth century Collector's Room, crammed full of clocks, paintings and art nouveau items such as vases. On the second floor, the apartment of a late nineteenth century Kraków bourgeois family has been faithfully reconstructed with some items such as fashionable magazines deliberately left lying around as if the inhabitants have just popped out for a while. Much of the furniture is of a heavy German style known as *Biedermeier*, which was popular at the time with the well-to-do of continental Europe. In the hallway of the apartment there are suitcases, a hatbox, a clothes hanger and a device to help people take off their shoes; the rooms supposedly belonging to the grandmother and one of her granddaughters are restrained and intimate, while the parlour, designed to show off the wealth of the family to visitors, is ostentatious, with china figurines in a glazed cabinet, framed photographs on the piano and walls adorned with ornate tapestries and family portraits.

are chains, a rare survival of an ancient city-wide system of crowd control.

There are two museums on Floriańska, a little further on from the Pod Różą and on the opposite (right hand) side. The **Muzeum Farmacji** at no.23 houses a collection of ancient medical paraphernalia, most of it in the forms of bottles and receptacles of all different shapes and sizes which gives the appearance of having escaped from a potions classroom at Harry Potter's school, Hogwarts. The museum is mostly seen on guided tours, but if there aren't enough people around, visitors can look round on their own, using the handy little green cards in each room, written in English, to guide them. Those with an interest in the history of science and medicine will want to linger the longest. Further on, on the same side of the road, the more substantial **Matejko House** forms the most worthwhile museum this street; it celebrates the work of Jan Matejko (1838 – 1893), one of the most important figures in the history of Polish art (see p.38).

Looming at the north end of Floriańska is the **Floriańska Gate** *(Brama Floriańska)*, one of the original medieval gateways into the city. It was built in 1307 to replace the first gate that stood here, which was constructed from wood and earthworks; a bas-relief on the tower shows St Florian, the patron saint of fire brigades (and of Kraków itself), who is using a pitcher of water to extinguish a fire. Inside the

The Matejko House Museum

Jan Matejko was director of the Kraków Academy of Fine Art during the nineteenth century. His vast paintings depicting important historical events in Polish history can be seen in the Sukiennice Art Gallery. Matejko trained in Vienna and Munich and for the whole of his life Kraków was part of the Austrian Empire, which is why Poland's past military glories often form the subject matter for his work. Matejko was born in this house and later lived here with his wife and family. His private rooms on the first floor have been left unchanged since his death, while his studio on the top floor is full of the curiosities he collected, including medieval torture instruments unearthed from the site of the Old Town Hall.

The place is very hushed and reverential towards the great man (who is referred to as "The Master" on a couple of occasions). Apart from Matejko's private collections there are of course examples of his work, including sketches he prepared for the stained glass windows of the Mariacki church; but perhaps the most absorbing thing about the museum is that the interior of the house has been preserved more or less the same as it was at Matejko's death in 1893, so you get a good idea of how prominent Cracovians lived during the nineteenth century. Much of the furniture is Italian, although some of the chairs are made from mother-of-pearl and come from the Middle East. A wander round the building's creaking floors takes visitors to the room where Matejko was born, and the room in which he died fifty-five years later, which was once his wife's "boudoir" – the ceiling awash with stars shining from a dark blue heaven, in a less expansive but more intimate echo of the ceiling in St Mary's Church.

tower is a small shrine to the Virgin Mary (with a late Baroque copy of the miraculous Icon known as the Madonna of the Sands) and just beyond it you can glimpse the brick **Barbican** fort (which the tour returns to after the Czartoryski Museum). The area to the left of the gate, alongside a restored part of the wall opposite the Polski Hotel, is a venue for the selling of some really kitsch paintings, tempting only for their awfulness. Here the crowd thins out, and beyond the paintings and the hotel you swing slightly to the left and pass under Kraków's own version of the **Bridge of Sighs**, which is part of the Czartoryski Museum (it has to be said that similar structures in Venice, Oxford and Cambridge are rather more appealing than this one). The entrance to the museum itself (see p.40) is round the corner to the left.

From the Piarist Church to the Holy Cross Church

Adjacent to the armoury building of the Czartoryski Museum is the museum's Armoury building is the Church of the Holy Transfiguration, the **Piarist Church**, a hulking baroque building and one of the few city centre churches whose doors are usually locked. Its designer was Kacper Bazanka who was an architect and a mayor of Kraków. Work began on the church in 1718; its rococo exterior dates from later in the century and is the work of an Italian architect, Placidi (it was during this era that so many churches were built in Kraków in Italian style that the city became known as the "Little Rome"). The Piarist order of monks, whose church this is, was founded in Spain in the early seventeenth century by St Joseph Calasanz (Calasanctius). It is a teaching order and St Joseph is patron saint of Roman Catholic schools; the monks of the order take four vows – poverty, chastity, obedience and special care of youth. If you manage to get inside, the most striking feature is the painted ceiling in the nave, designed to give the illusion that the building is longer and airier than it actually is. An urn near the altar contains the heart of an education reformer, Stanislaw Konarski, who was a member of the Piarist order; you can see a bust of him above the main entrance to the church.

Opposite the church is a smart hotel, the *Francuski*, a refined and quiet haven for a filling (but expensive) lunch. It is the sort of place where people start frowning if you accidentally drop your fork, but the food is very good and the location, tucked away on the side of a quiet square, is a fine one.

Round the back of the Piarist Church is part of the **Planty**, the ring of greenery which surrounds the old city and which is modelled loosely on the Ringstrasse in Vienna. The planty follows the line of the former city walls which were established in 1285 when the right of the city to be surrounded by fortifications was given by Duke

The Adam Mickiewicz statue in the main square: education symbolised by the tutoring of a young boy

Hotel Pod Różą

The hotel has been at no.14 Floriańska since the eighteenth century and its guests have included Tsar Alexander I and the composer Franz Liszt. There is a Latin inscription above the sixteenth century portal which reads: "Let this house survive until an ant drinks the whole of the seas and a tortoise walks all around the world." Inside, the hotel is built around a glassed-in courtyard and will charge you at least $100 per night for a room. The pricey restaurant serves excellent Polish food (see pages 129 and 149 for more details).

The Czartoryski Museum (Muzeum

The Czartoryski Museum is the oldest art-historical museum in Poland. It was founded in 1801 by Izabela Czartoryska, the wife of Prince Adam Czartoryski, at their family estate at Pulawy near Warsaw. The collection that Izabela had assembled was moved to Paris in 1830 (following an insurrection against Russian occupation of Poland, in which the family was implicated) and finished up in Kraków in 1876. Nazi occupation led to the loss or destruction of several valuable exhibits, including Raphael's *Portrait of a Young Man*, which remains lost to this day. In 1991 Adam Czartoryski, a member of the museum's founding family, regained control of the collection from the Polish State (and donated it back to the nation).

The collection now includes Roman, Egyptian and Polish historical artefacts, and Flemish, Dutch, Italian and Polish art (including works by Rembrandt and Leonardo da Vinci). It is spread through three linked buildings, the Palace, the Monastery and the Armoury. The main ticket office, on the ground floor of the Palace, is on ulica św. Jana.

The Palace

As you head upstairs you will pass shields of honour dedicated to Polish kings and military commanders. The first floor includes Persian carpets and oriental scimitars, trophies retrieved from the Turkish army as they retreated from the siege of Vienna in 1683; here there is also enamelware from France and Italy, German silverware, Venetian glassware, seventeenth century furniture from Spain

Leszek the Black. Once there were eight main gates and forty-six towers; now only the Floriańska gate, the three gates near it, and the walls that link them, survive. The near-by gates are named the Tailors' Gate, the Joiners' Gate and the Carpenters' gate, after the guilds that were assigned to maintain their defence. The Planty itself is the filled-in moat that once surrounded the walls. Sprinkled with fountains, lakes and refreshment stalls, it's a cool haven in summer, a shady retreat from nearby bustling streets such as Floriańska. In winter, people shuffle along its icy paths while children dodge between the stark, lifeless trees, throwing snowballs or sledging down grassy banks.

The most obvious feature in this part of the Planty is the bastion known as

rtoryskich)

Below left: Kraków's own version of the Venetian "Bridge of Sighs" links two parts of the Czartoryski Museum

and Bohemia, Dresden china figures and portraits of prominent Polish figures, including those connected with the Czartoryski family.

The second floor forms the gallery of European Painting, including medieval triptychs from Italy, Poland and the Low Countries, and French, Italian, German and Flemish sixteenth and seventeenth century portraiture and landscapes, the best of which is Rembrandt's sombre, brooding *Landscape with the Good Samaritan*. The gallery's most famous painting is Leonardo da Vinci's *Lady with an Ermine*, in a small alcove all on its own to allow silent, reverential gazing. The lady concerned is one Cecilia Gallerani, the mistress of Leonardo's patron, Duke Lodovico Sforza; the animal she holds is either an ermine (a reference to the duke's nickname) or a weasel (in Greek gale, which might be a reference to the woman's name). Other paintings to look out for in these galleries include *Portrait of a Boy* by the seventeenth century Dutch artist Caspar Netscher, and *Madonna and Child* by Vincenzo Catena, another highlight of the museum's collection of Italian art.

The Monastery and the Armoury

An imitation of the Bridge of Sighs in Venice links the second floor of the Palace to the Monastery. There's much less to grab the attention here: armoury, swords and Polish art adorn the walls, including Jan Matejko's sentimental *Poland in Chains*, and elsewhere you can see furniture and yet more portraits. Linked to the monastery by a passageway, the Armoury contains items from Roman, Greek and Egyptian civilisations. Most noteworthy are the second century AD mosaic depicting Hercules fighting with the Cretan bull, some fabulous Greek vases, Etruscan sarcophagi with portraits of the deceased incumbents on the lids, and Egyptian sarcophagi dating from around 2000 BC, with canopic jars (for storage of the intestines and other bodily parts) nearby. Other parts of the Armoury provide exhibition space for seventeenth century tapestries and sculptures depicting classical themes.

the **Barbican** *(Barbakan)*, built in 1498 after King Jan Olbracht was defeated by the Turks at Bukowina and felt that they were a threat to Kraków. However, the first attackers to be repelled by forces stationed here were the Habsburgs, who unsuccessfully laid siege to the city in 1587. The building was supposedly inspired by Arab military architecture (the name may also be derived from the Arabic *bal-baqara*, meaning the gate to a barn – although one Kraków historian has suggested that it derives from the Latin *barba*, meaning a beard, the name alluding to it being an appendage to the defensive walls). The building is surrounded by *bartizans*, small lookout towers, of which there are seven – a supposedly mystical number. The top gallery of the building has windows from which boiling tar or stones could be directed at attackers; however the Barbican was built at the time when gunpowder weapons were being developed, and the lower galleries were intended for artillery defence. In 1768 defenders in the Barbican fought back the Russian advance on the city, and a plaque in the building commemorates Marcin Oraczewski who, according to legend, killed the Russian general with a button fired from his gun after his supply of bullets had run out.

The structure was formerly connected to the Floriańska Gate by means of a drawbridge which crossed a moat; nothing remains today of either. Not particularly graceful, the building is nonetheless the largest and best-preserved medieval barbican in Europe; by the eighteenth century it had become derelict and redundant, but suggestions made by the Austrian Emperor Franz II to knock it down were refuted by Feliks Radwanski, a Professor at the Jagiellonian University, who said that the Barbican protected the city from chilly northerly winds, which would otherwise (he claimed) cause "delicately-bred" women and children to succumb to gum disease and rheumatism. Although there is not much to see inside the Barbican, there are good views from the galleries that circle the interior of the building at various levels, and the coliseum-like structure makes the place a good venue for pageants and historical re-enactments. Just beyond the building, to the east, the Planty opens out, with the railway station over to the left, and the ochre-hued **Słowacki Theatre** on the right.

The theatre was completed in 1893 and is named after the Romantic playwright Julius Słowacki (whose funeral casket lay in state in the Barbican when he died in 1927). It is modelled on the Paris Opera; its architect, Jan Zawiejski, had studied in Vienna and Paris and the theatre clearly evokes grand nineteenth century buildings in those cities. The facade, along plac sw. Ducha, is lined with figures that represent poetry, drama, comedy, song, dance, joy and sadness, along with two figures from *Pan Tadeusz*, the epic poem by Mickiewicz (see p.28). The inscription, *Kraków narodowej Sztuce*, translates as "Kraków's gift to national art". The theatre is the principal venue in the city for ballet and opera. In November 2006 performances here included *Die Fledermaus* by Johann Strauss and Donizetti's *Don Pasquale*. Part of the summer opera and operetta festival take places here and classical concerts and recitals are also occasionally given. The auditorium is particularly sumptuous, with a stage curtain that depicts Apollo striking an agreement between Beauty and Love, surrounded by many other allegorical figures. The box offices for plays and opera performances have separate entrances on either side of the main entrance to the building.

Next door to the theatre on plac św. Ducha is the russet-brick **Holy Cross Church**, its front, like the theatre's, looking out over a small area of greenery. A wooden church was founded here in the early thirteenth century, and this original building soon found its way into the hands of the neighbouring Hospital of the Holy Spirit (knocked down in 1892 to make way for the theatre); the hospital's symbol, a double cross, can be seen in many parts of the church. The current building dates from the fourteenth century. It is a bright, airy church, the absence of stained glass lending its interior a feeling of spaciousness which other Kraków churches lack. Inside there's an unusual architectural flourish dating from the 1520s: a single pillar in the centre of the church is all that supports the late Gothic palm vaulting. The frescoes (or what's left of them) date from the fifteenth and sixteenth centuries.

Along Ulica Szpitalna to Mały Rynek

Ulica Szpitalna runs south from the theatre and the church, parallel with Floriańska but a world away from it in character. It is quiet and subdued along here, with small book and food shops forming the main retail outlets. Most of the buildings which line the street are nineteenth century mansions; the most ornate of these, half way along on the left, is now occupied by a bank.

At number 21, just after the Holy Cross Church, a Gothic building on the left houses the idiosyncratic collection of the **Theatre Museum**, where theatrical programmes, costumes and set designs are on display. Most of the exhibits are associated with the Słowacki Theatre, such as the old sepia photos of absurdly moustachioed performers noted for their playing in Shakespearean tragedies in the nineteenth century; other exhibits include the puppets used in the daringly satirical cabaret shows of the early twentieth century, and photographs recalling the heyday of the Cricot 2 Theatre in Kraków, where in the 1960s avant-garde stage shows were developed by the visionary director Tadeusz Kantor. At number 24, on the right around thirty metres further on, is the city's **Orthodox Church**, situated in a building which was a synagogue until 1939. The church occupies the upstairs floor of what looks like an ordinary house, and is known for its interior design by the artist Jerzy Nowosielski, one of Poland's most important post-war artists; his distinctly modernist ideas reflect Byzantine and other much older influences.

Beyond here the street opens out into **Mały Rynek**, a quiet square overlooked by the towers of St Mary's but vastly less busy than the Rynek Główny. The name translates as "Small Market Square" and in medieval times this place was crammed with shops and stalls selling meat and fish, although in the eighteenth century it became the city's fruit and vegetable market. The unpressurised pace of things here makes a stop at one of the cafes on the left-hand side of the square worthwhile, particularly in summer when there are opportunities to eat or drink outside. Opposite the restaurants are two shops, much visited by nuns, selling all manner of church vestments and other devotional paraphernalia which the less charitable might be tempted to condemn as "kitsch"; whatever your own views are on what is on offer, the shops seem to do a roaring trade, in everything from priest's robes and devotional painting of the Virgin Mary to Pope John Paul II calendars and porcelain models of the Baby Jesus.

The Dominican and Franciscan Churches

Ulica Stolarska runs off the south part of the Mały Rynek, curving around past the German, American and French Consulates towards the hulking mass of the **Dominican Church** (*Kościół Dominikanow)*. The church is largely a nineteenth century construction, incorporating Gothic characteristics of earlier churches built on this site, including the building which stood here until a disastrous fire in 1850. The facade, topped with a myriad of pinnacles, is an appropriate introduction to the building, which was conceived on a grandiose scale.

The oldest of many side chapels in the church is that of St Jacek, reached by a flight of stone steps on the north wall (on the left as you enter). Jacek died in 1257 and was the monastery's first prior. His tomb was a venerated site of pilgrimage for many centuries. The present appearance of the chapel dates from around 1700. Over the stairs are two huge paintings by Tomasso Dolabella, *The Last Supper and The Wedding at Cana*; unfortunately both are very gloomy and the images on them are indistinct. In the tomb itself there is much effusive stucco work (by Baldassare Fontana) and if you find the door under the stone flight of stairs unlocked, you can take a peek at the Gothic cloisters, lined with Renaissance tombstones that mark the resting places of rich city burghers. On the opposite side of the nave to the Chapel of St Jacek is the domed Myszkowski Chapel, built between 1603 and 1614 for a rich local family, whose busts form part of the decoration of the dome; next to it is the tomb of Prospero Provano (died 1584), a businessman who made his money in

Dominicans and Franciscans

The Dominican order was founded in 1215, with the first monastic houses established in Toulouse and Oxford soon after. There have been Dominican monks in Kraków since 1237 and nowadays there's reckoned to be a global community of around ten thousand Dominican monks and nuns. For many centuries the order was associated with a rather fearsome reputation, basking proudly in the nickname given to it by monks of other orders, *domini canes*, "the dogs of the Lord". Dominicans formulated the Spanish Inquisition and later became the intellectual elite of the church. In the 1980s the order in Kraków was associated with student protest, and became a focal point for an orthodox Catholic revival that antagonised the communist authorities.

The Franciscan Order, founded by St Francis of Assisi in 1209, has split into many factions since then. There has been a Franciscan monastery in Kraków since 1240, and for over seven centuries the two orders whose churches face each other across plac Dominikańska have competed for influence in the city. The Franciscan Church is very busy nowadays, with many services held here and many social and pastoral activities performed by its priests.

the salt trade, who is portrayed lying recumbent on his tomb.

Outside the church, **Dominikańska** is a narrow street, busy with traffic and trams; it's another reference point in central Kraków, and is always busy with people walking along Grodzka, which links the Rynek Główny with Wawel.

Across the square you can see the **Franciscan Church**, whose construction began in 1255 when this location lay just outside the city walls. The founder of the Church was Bolesław the Chaste, the medieval duke who drew up the ground plan for the city centre. In 1386 the pagan Grand Duke of Lithuania, Jogaila, was baptised in this church and as Władysław Jagiełło became the first Christian king of Poland. Further rebuilding of the church took place in the ensuing centuries and the place is now a gloomier and more sombre affair than the Dominican house of worship. There's an aura of mysticism about the place, augmented by the heavy presence of incense and by the murals and stained glass, most of which date from around 1900 following the reconstruction of the church after the nineteenth century fire (which devastated much of this area, including the Dominican Church).

The window above the main entrance, built by the admired artist Stanisław Wyspiański in 1900 and entitled *God the Father Creating the World* is a whirling, misty but intensely beautiful and vivid array of abstract colours that depict God emerging from the cosmic chaos. There are planets, recently created, falling from God's cloak, while peacock feathers from local folk-costumes are also incorporated into the design, which is reckoned to be one of the most significant examples of the art nouveau style in Poland. Wyspiański also designed the murals that adorn the walls of the church, many of which are brightly coloured and feature flowers, conveying the Franciscan love of nature. And there is another of his stained glass windows behind the altar: St Francis is depicted with the Blessed Salomea (the wife of Bołesław the Chaste) and representations of the four elements, earth, air, fire and water. Salomea herself rejected the coronet that came with her position as the wife of a duke; instead she took holy orders and became a Poor Clare nun.

The chapels which lead off from the side of the building's single nave contain various objects of devotion. Most famous is a Gothic representation of the Virgin Mary *(Mater Dolorosa)* in the north chapel. The Virgin wears a heavy, ornate crown and is surrounded by angels holding instruments of Christ's passion. A painting, dating from 1970, depicts the martyr Maksymilian Kolbe, a Polish priest who chose to die in the Auschwitz concentration camp in the place of another, and was later canonized (his prison number is shown in the lower right of the picture). From the south side of the church you should be able to reach the cloisters, including their portraits of Kraków bishops dating back to the year 1400. Across the road from the church is the palace of the archbishops of Kraków, occupied from 1964 to 1978 by one Karol Wojtyła (see p.107).

From the church it's easy to get back to the Rynek Główny along Bracka or the busier Grodzka, which like Floriańska is lined with shops and restaurants.

Arches, walkways & wall plaques; splendid architectural details of the Jagiellonian University

The University District

Kraków has an academic tradition that stretches back over six hundred years and is centred on the **Jagiellonian University**, whose ancient heart is situated along the southern end of **ulica Jagiellońska**, immediately west of the Rynek Główny. This traffic-free cobbled street, lined with tall, austere buildings, opens out onto an attractive area of the *Planty*. Overlooking the street is a distinctive medieval oriel window, whose high panes once provided daylight to lecturers who stood in the alcove it shelters, in front of classes of students struggling to write notes in the darkness of the room beyond.

The passageway almost directly below the oriel window marks the entrance to the courtyard of the **Collegium Maius**, whose construction (using red brick and pale limestone) in the 1490s was a result of the re-founding of the university by Władisław Jagiełło in 1400. Formerly housing the university library, the building now forms the **University Museum** and is used for university ceremonies and functions. Cloistered and secretive, it's a hushed retreat away from city centre activity, and is faintly reminiscent of the quad of a medieval Oxford college (although it's been much rebuilt over the ages and is essentially nineteenth century neo-Gothic). The well in the centre of the courtyard was built in 1958 and bears the coats of arms of Kraków, Anjou, Lithuania and Poland. The guttering is fashioned into gargoyle-type designs at each of the courtyard's four corners; on warm days in winter snowmelt spills continuously from the mouths of the grotesquely contorted faces. If you're here at 11am or 1pm you can watch the **procession of medieval figures** which appear beneath the main clock as it chimes the hour (after which the student hymn *Gaudeamus Igitur* is heard). Despite its looks and name, the clock and the figures are a modern feature, although the procession seems

The Jagiellonian University

The Jagiellonian University, the most prestigious in Poland (and second largest after the University of Warsaw) was founded by King Kazimierz the Great in 1364, making it one of the oldest universities in Europe (though its foundation post-dates that of the first Oxford and Cambridge colleges by more than a century). It was beset by problems during its early years. When Kazimierz died in 1370 there were barely any buildings, and the teaching was done in Wawel and in the private homes of academics. The monarch who succeeded Kazimierz was Louis the Hungarian, who wasn't interested in the *Academia Cracoviensis* as he was busy nurturing Hungary's own university in the town of Pécs. So the University of Kraków was more or less re-founded in the year 1400 by Louis's daughter, Queen Jadwiga, and her husband, King Właysław Jagiełło, after whom the institution is named. The university was established in the former Jewish quarter; the residents of that district were moved to another part of the city to make way for the buildings that now make up the heart of the university.

The university's earliest faculties were those of Ecclesiastical Law, Civil Law, Medicine and Science. In its early years it quickly gained a reputation as a centre for the study of astrology and alchemy; Dr Faustus, who died around 1538, is said to have studied here, and although there is no record of him doing so, the writer Goethe visited Kraków in 1790 while researching his play *Faust*. In 1583 Dr John Dee, court alchemist to Elizabeth I in England (and probably an English spy), came all the way to Kraków to consult the academics who were at that time considered world experts on the subject. Although Dee's visit was controversial, as he was the guest of Olbracht Laski, a nobleman who had conspired against the Polish King, the alchemist nonetheless made a mark on the place and left a gift to the university library – a manuscript of Boethius' *De Consolatione Philosophiae*.

The university has grown considerably through the centuries. This expansion has meant that many of the student halls of residence and academic faculties are nowadays spread through the city. A cluster of these modern buildings line al. Mickeiwicza, west of the Collegium Maius, and include the University Library, built in the 1930s, which houses thousands of rare books and manuscripts along with day-to-day books needed by students. In the twentieth century the institution's international reputation for science grew considerably: Karol Olszewski, who was the first scientist to produce stable liquid nitrogen and oxygen, was a Professor here just before World War One. (A short time later Karol Wojtyła, later Pope John Paul II, studied theology and Polish literature at the university.) The Nazis saw the place as a threat and sent most of the senior academics to the concentration camp of Sachsenhausen in 1939. After World War Two the Communist authorities tried to overshadow the intellectual power of the university by opening the huge Nowa Huta steelworks in the suburbs of Kraków, attempting to counterbalance the city's academic and intellectual reputation with a new industrial one. Since 1990, with post-communist Poland striving to make new headway on the international stage, the University has had an opportunity to build further on its international reputation – which is already over six centuries old.

Guided Tour of the Collegium Maius

If you want to get any further than the courtyard of the Collegium Maius, you'll need to join a guided tour, usually given in English once or twice a day; ask at the museum information centre for details of times or ring to book in advance on (012) 663 1307. The tour, which lasts around thirty minutes, is particularly worth taking if you have an interest in science or astronomy. You are taken first through a variety of reception rooms which blend the hushed, refined worlds of academe and ceremony; in the Great Hall (*Aula*), the main assembly hall, where a Renaissance ceiling with rosettes and portraits of royalty and benefactors, an inscription above the Renaissance portal reads *Plus Ratio Quam Vis* – "Wisdom Rather than Strength". Another striking room is the formal common room and dining room, the *Stuba Communis*, with its beautiful Renaissance ceiling, fourteenth century statue of Kazimierz the Great, and ornate wooden curving staircase built in Danzig (Gdańsk) in the seventeenth century. The most important collections are the medieval scientific instruments in the Treasury, where a tiny copper globe, fashioned in 1510 as part of a much larger astronomical and time-keeping device, was the first in the world to show the continent of North America (although it is marked as being in the southern hemisphere!). Also on display here, slightly incongruously, are a set of eleventh century astrolabes, fashioned in the Spanish city of Cordoba when it was under Arab rule, and the awards given to Polish film director Andrzej Wajda at the Cannes and Venice film festivals (the Golden Palm and the Golden Lion respectively) which he has donated to the museum.

to attract a predictably enthusiastic camera-clicking crowd of onlookers. The guided tour of the rooms making up the Collegium Maius (see p.49) is well worth taking, while on the ground floor of the building is a separate exhibition full of interactive science experiments.

Close by on św. Anny is **St Anne's Church**, built between 1689 and 1703 as the University Church, and one of the biggest Baroque buildings in the city. Its designer was a Dutch architect, Tylman van Gameren; the striking stucco decoration and statues are the work of an Italian sculptor, Baltasare Fontana. It's a burial place for university bigwigs (the church is hung with black flags when a professor dies), and also provides the venue for ceremonial events and the marriages of former students. The high, central dome and fine murals make this one of the most highly regarded Baroque churches in Kraków, the lack of stained glass in the windows giving it an airy brightness which many of the city's gloomier churches lack. On the right hand wall of the church is the shrine of Jan Kanty (John of Kęty), a university professor of theology during the fifteenth century who was later canonized and is the

Andrzej Wajda

Though the first domestic film was shot back in 1908, Polish cinema only really came of age in the 1950s, and this was due mainly to the achievements of Andrzej Wajda whose international awards are on show in the Collegium Maius. Born in 1926 in Suwalki, Wajda studied painting at the Kraców Academy of Fine Arts for three years before jumping creative ship and heading to lódz where Poland's only film school was situated. The three films that make up Wajda's famous war trilogy (*A Generation, Canal and Ashes and Diamonds*) are all reflections on the devastation of World War II on Poland and unsentimentalized monuments to the heroism of ordinary people during those difficult days (Wajda himself fought for the Resistance). Despite his instant international reputation Wajda has remained the most Polish of directors, adapting many of his country's established literary classics for the large screen – including Wyspiański's *The Wedding* – though in a way always conscious of their relevance to the present. In 2000 Andrzej Wajda received an Oscar for lifetime achievement; he presently lives in Kraców.

university's patron saint (his old rooms in the Collegium Maius are now a small chapel). The saint's relics are in a sarcophagus supported by figures representing the faculties of the ancient university – theology, philosophy, law and medicine. On top of the columns surrounding the sarcophagus are other Saint Johns – St John the Baptist, St John the Evangelist, St John Chrysostom, and St John Damascene.

The nineteenth century **Collegium Novum** on ul. Golębia is an austere nineteenth century neo-Gothic building which is the present seat of the university's directorate and administration offices. You are unlikely to be able to see inside (the central courtyard is modelled on the Collegium Maius; the main hall known as the *Aula Magna*, whose walls are lined with paintings of kings and scholars, provides a venue for chamber concerts). At the front of the building, surrounded by trees, you can see a statue of former university student **Nicolaus Copernicus** (1473 – 1543). The statue dates from 1900 and was originally intended to be a fountain. The young scholar is portrayed holding a medieval astrolabe in his hands. (see also p.50).

More Art Galleries

If your appetite for art has not been satiated by the Czartoryski Museum, there are four further galleries in the city you might want to explore. A short walk west of the university district, on al 3 Maja and opposite the huge Cracovia Hotel, the National Museum (Muzeum Narodowe) houses a permanent collection of weapons and military uniforms but is better-known as a gallery of Modern Polish Art, which occupies the second (uppermost) floor. Labelling in these galleries is in English and displays cover a variety of media, including short films, sculptures, paintings and other

Copernicus

Nicolaus Copernicus (1473 – 1543), Mikołaj Kopernik to the Poles, was born in Toruń, a town on the Wisła in north-west Poland. His family were merchants with strong church connections. Between 1491 and 1495 Copernicus was supposedly a student at the Jagiellonian University (although the only firm evidence that he actually studied here is an entry made in a university payments book); like most intellectuals of his day, he also travelled abroad, later studying at the universities of Bologna and Padua. He was a doctor, lawyer and soldier, and spent fifteen years as a canon of a church in Frombork, a town on Poland's Baltic coast. Here he built an observatory, and his studies led to his most famous and radical idea – that the earth went round the sun, and not the other way round. So heretical were his theories that at first he only circulated them around his fellow scientists. However Pope Paul III urged him to publish the ideas and eventually Copernicus's treatise *On the Revolutions of the Heavenly Spheres* was published (in Nuremberg) in the year that he died; after its publication the Catholic Church changed its mind and the volume was placed on the index of banned books from 1616 to 1835 (Martin Luther also disapproved, calling Copernicus "a fool…for trying to reverse the science of astronomy").

installations. Symbolist works such as Wojciech Weiss's *Self Portrait with Masks*, in which the artist has portrayed himself carrying a collection of strikingly distorted heads, and Jacek Malczewski's *Nike of the Legions* are worth looking out for. The latter shows Nike, the goddess of Victory, sitting over the body of a Roman legionary who resembles the legendary military commander and politician Józef Piłsudski. This leading figure in twentieth century Polish history was made Head of State in 1918 after being imprisoned by the Germans; soon afterwards he led a hard-won military campaign against the Russians that rewarded him with a state funeral and burial in Wawel Cathedral when he died in 1935 (his grey tunic, forming part of his army uniform, can be seen in the military collection on the ground floor). Also look out for Stanisław Wyspiański's designs for the stained glass windows in Wawel Cathedral (a design entitled Polonia) and the design by the Cubist artist Zbigniew Pronaszko for a never-completed statue of Adam Mickiewicz (see p.28) in Vilnius. The first floor of the museum houses a good collection of decorative arts, including stained glass from Kraków's churches and robes worn by Polish artistocrats in the seventeenth century. Space on the ground floor is also given over to visiting exhibitions and it is possible to buy tickets for selected parts of the museum, or for all of it. The imposing building housing these diverse collections is a brutal, graceless structure that looks as if it might date from Communist times but is in fact slightly older, having been constructed in 1934.

A stylish pavilion built in 1994 on the south bank of the river, with a fine view

The Wyspiański Museum and the Bunker of Art

Stanisław Wyspiański was a multi-talented resident of Kraków who died of ill-health in 1907 at the tender age of thirty-eight. Famed for his experiments in playwriting, poetry and painting (and he even tried his hand at typography and costume and furniture design), he is probably best known for his play *The Wedding (Wesele)* written in 1901, which he based on the real-life wedding of one of his Cracovian poet friends to a local peasant girl; a deeply melancholic work, the play lays bare the social divisions of the Polish people and, as the atmosphere gets more surreal, several figures from Polish history turn up to bring into focus the impotence of the Polish nationalist movement (at the time of writing Poland as a country didn't exist). The play has since become a Polish classic and was turned into a film by Andrzej Wajda.

The Wyspiański Museum in Szołayski House at pl.Szczepański 11, 100m northwest of the Rynek Główny, is not primarily a literary one, however, but rather concerned with his paintings, engravings and designs for stained glass windows (Wyspiański's executed work can be seen in the Franciscan church, page 45). As a painter his talent lay in portraiture, especially in the depiction of children either sleeping or in rare quiet mode.

On the same square as the Wyspiański Museum is the **Bunker of Art** *(Bunkier Sztuki)* at pl.Szczepanski 3 (www.bunkier.com.pl), an art gallery specializing in contemporary art with an ever-changing programme of exhibitions.

across to Wawel, houses a **collection of Japanese art**, with both permanent and temporary collections, mainly of characteristic Japanese woodcuts, prints, Samurai armour and textiles. The building was paid for by Andrzej Wajda, the oscar-winning film director, and designed by a Japanese architect, Arata Isozaki. Most of the exhibits were collected by Feliks Jasieński (1861-1929), a leading Japanologist whose nickname was "Manggha" (from the Japanese word 'manga' which means 'sketch'). The exhibition is not large, but it's spaciously and effectively housed, and the café, which spills out onto an attractive terrace in Summer, is very pleasant, with Japanese food on offer and a splendid view of the river. The gallery's official title is *Centrum Sztuki I Techniki Japońskiej Manggha* and its address is ul.Konopnickiej 26; to get there, cross the Grundwaldzskie bridge and it's the low-slung grey building on the right. Tram 18 runs there from the junction of Dominkańska and Grodzka in the city centre.

Places to visit in the Old Town

Museums and Galleries

Czartoryski Museum

North end of ul.św.Jana
Open: May-Oct, Tue-Sun, 10am-4pm (Tue,Thu), 7pm (Wed,Fri,Sat), 3pm (Sun); Nov-Apr, Tue-Sun, 10am -3.30pm (Tue,Thu,Sat,Sun), 6pm (Wed,Fri)

Wyspiański (Szołayski House Collection)

plac Szczepanski 9
Open: Tues–Sun 10am–3pm (5:30pm Fri)

National Museum

Al 3 Maja 1 (opposite Cracovia Hotel)
Open: Tues–Sun 10am–3:30pm (until 6pm Weds)

Gallery of Nineteenth Century Polish Art

Sukiennice (Cloth-hall), Rynek Główny
Open: Tue-Sun 10am–3:30pm (6pm Thu)

Hipoliti House

Pl. Mariacki 3
Open: May-Oct, Wed-Sun, 10am-5.30pm, Nov-Apr, Wed-Sun 9am – 4pm (noon-7pm Thu); closed the second Sunday of each month throughout the year

Historical Museum

North-west corner of Rynek Główny (no 35)
Open: May-Oct, Wed-Sun, 10am-5.30pm; Nov-Apr, Wed-Sun, 9am-4pm Wed-Sun; closed second Sunday of each month throughout the year

Jan Matejko Museum

Floriańska 41
Open: Tue–Sun, 10am–3:30pm (6pm Fri)

Pharmacy Museum (Muzeum Farmacji)

Floriańska 23
Open: Tues 3pm–7pm; Wed–Sun 11am–2pm

Theatre Museum

Szpitalna 21
Open: Wed 11am–6pm; Thu–Sun 9am–3:30pm

Churches and other attractions

The following churches (with the exception of the Piarist Church) are open most of the time, although there is no tourist access during services (which are frequent, especially on Sun).

St Mary's (the Mariacki Church)

Rynek Główny: church open from 11.30am daily (from 2pm Sun and Saints Days); Veit Stoss altar shown daily except Sunday and Saints Days at 11:50am; church closes to visitors at 6pm.

Dominican Church

plac Dominikańska.

Franciscan Church

Franciszkanska.

St Adalbert's

Rynek Główny.

Piarist Church

ul.Pijarska.

Holy Cross Church

plac sw.Ducha.

Barbican

North end of Floriańska, through the Floriańska Gate
Open 10.30am–6pm daily

Wieza Ratuszowa (the town hall tower)

Rynek Glówny
Open: 10.30am–6pm daily; visiting hours may be curtailed in winter

Collegium Maius (ancient part of the Jagiellonian University of Kraków)

ul.Jagiellonska
Access on guided tours only;
book in advance, in person or on: ☎ (012) 663 1307
Open 10am–2pm (Sat), 3pm (Mon, Wed, Fri), 6pm (Tue, Thu). Last visitors admitted 40 minutes before closing time

2. Wawel - The Castle & Cathedral

The Route to Wawel

This tour takes us from the commercial hub of Kraków, centred on Rynek Główny, to its spiritual heart, Wawel Hill, site of the city's cathedral and royal castle. If you're in a hurry you might want to press straight on to the castle; but for those with time to spare, exploration of the picturesque streets and squares between the Rynek and Wawel is very worthwhile - and the area is choc-full of restaurants, from the familiar offerings of the local Pizza Hut to those serving Ukrainian and Hungarian fare.

Left: Wawel, seen from the south bank of the Wisła

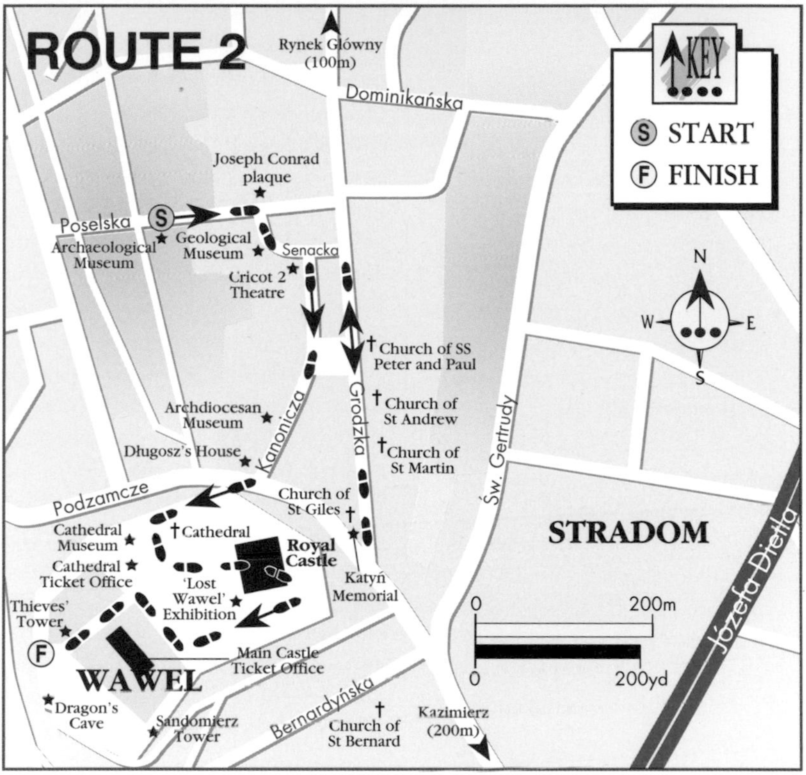

ROUTE 2

Rynek Główny (100m)
Dominikańska
KEY
S START
F FINISH
Joseph Conrad plaque
Poselska
Archaeological Museum
Geological Museum
Senacka
Cricot 2 Theatre
Church of SS Peter and Paul
Church of St Andrew
Church of St Martin
Grodzka
Kanonicza
Archdiocesan Museum
Długosz's House
Św. Gertrudy
N
W
E
S
Podzamcze
Church of St Giles
Cathedral
Cathedral Museum
Cathedral Ticket Office
Royal Castle
Katyń Memorial
STRADOM
'Lost Wawel' Exhibition
Thieves' Tower
Main Castle Ticket Office
WAWEL
Dragon's Cave
Sandomierz Tower
Bernardyńska
Church of St Bernard
Kazimierz (200m)
0 200m
0 200yd
Józefa Dietla

The Archaeological Museum

The city's **Archaeological Museum** (*Muzeum Archeologiczne*), at Poselska 3, is housed in a rather grand building, a former palace which served the Austrians as a prison and court complex during the nineteenth century; it was handed over to the Department of Antiquities at the end of the Second World War. You enter the complex via its expansive gardens, which provide a small haven of peace in the city centre.

The ground floor is usually set aside for temporary exhibitions, while upstairs there are permanent displays covering prehistoric Nowa Huta, ancient and medieval Małopolska (the local area) and ancient Egypt. The Egyptian selection is relatively small but very well presented and features a number of interesting sarcophagi and mummies (don't be afraid to enter the darkened rooms - the lights only go on when there is someone in them). Elsewhere, the museum appears mainly designed for schoolchildren - the emphasis being not so much on artefacts as scale models, dummies and computer simulations. However, one grand exception to this, standing pride of place in the museum's collection, is a tall (and very rare) stone statue of the four-faced pagan Slav god Światowid, which is thought to date from around the tenth century (it was found in 1848 in the River Zbrucz in the Ukraine). The museum ends with a short display on the history of the museum itself, partially labelled in English.

Exit the museum and turn right down Poselska. On the building across the road from the T-junction with Senacka you will see a stone plaque commemorating the writer **Joseph Conrad** (1857-1924), who lived in Kraków from 1869-74 (this was one of his addresses); although Conrad wrote his novels in English, the dedication is in Polish only. Conrad was a remarkably prolific writer who used to keep several books on the go at once. His novel *Heart of Darkness*, published in 1899, is generally regarded as being the first novel of the twentieth century.

Along Kanoniczna Street to the Church of Saints Peter and Paul

Turn now into the narrow street Senacka; located just past the administrative offices of the Archaeological Museum is the city's tiny **Geological Museum** *(Muzeum Geologiczna)* - the staff here are very friendly and a booklet in English is available, but unless you're really very interested in rocks there's not too much of interest on display. From here walk down **Kanoniczna**, one of Kraków's oldest and most picturesque streets. During the last decade many of the buildings on the street have finally undergone some form of facelift after years of neglect during the communist era, when the conservation of buildings was very low on the list of municipal priorities.

At number 5 is the **Cricot 2 Theatre** (*Cricoteka*) which in July and August houses an exhibition dedicated to the work of Tadeusz Kantor (1915-90), the Polish avant-garde actor and theatre director who founded the theatre in 1956. Kantor was a graduate of the Kraków Academy of Fine Arts and he initially gained recognition as a painter; he established his first theatre company during World War Two (a venture punishable by death at the time) and at the Cricot 2 Theatre he worked as writer, director, choreographer, costumer, set designer and just about everything else. Renowned for their surreal sets, dreamlike atmospheres and unpredictable "happenings", Kantor's plays eventually toured the globe and received universal acclaim. The nature of the exhibition changes from year to year; at the time of writing it was a collection of his pen and ink drawings. If you are curious to see what's on display, you can buy a ticket from the office situated to the left as you enter.

St Mary Magdalene Square

Walk down Kanoniczna to the open square, known as St Mary Magdalene Square, dominated by the glorious facade of the **Church of Saints Peter and Paul** (*Kościół Św Piotra i Pawła*) which was founded by King Zygmunt III and modelled on the Jesuit Church of *Il Gesú* (in Rome) - it is considered one of the most important examples

Joseph Conrad

Joseph Conrad (Teodor Józef Konrad Korzeniowski) is regarded as one of the great English writers, yet though he wrote his novels in English he was born in Berdychev (now in the Ukraine) and spent his formative years in Kraków - indeed English was his fourth language after Russian, Polish and French. Mainly renowned for his tales of the sea and his studies of the strange psychological effects of journeys to exotic parts, Conrad worked for many years as a merchant seaman and it seems that writing for him was not something that came particularly easy; he called the completion of his book *Nostromo* "an achievement upon which my friends may congratulate me as upon recovery from a dangerous illness". Conrad became a British subject in 1886 and he died in England in 1924. However, he did once return to Kraków in 1914 with his wife and two sons in order that they would know something of his roots. Critics generally point to either *Nostromo* or *Heart of Darkness* (which formed the basis for the film *Apocalypse Now*) as his finest work but also worth seeking out is his *A Personal Record*, a semi-autobiographical story about his early life as a Pole living in a country that at the time was divided between Russia, Austria and Prussia.

of the early Baroque style in central Europe. The statue in the middle of the square is of Piotr Skarga Pawęski (1536-1612), one of the leading lights of the Jesuit movement in Poland who wrote the highly influential *Lives of the Saints* and served as King Zygmunt III's confessor for 24 years. A nearby modern water fountain provides some comic relief as children of all ages attempt to reach the spurting water without getting soaked up to their knees, while the square's southern side is occupied by one of the most austerely housed Pizza Huts you'll ever see.

The Church of Saints Peter and Paul is heroically prefaced by magnificent statutes of the twelve Apostles; they date originally from the early eighteenth century, though what you see today are copies (to protect the originals from the heavily polluted Cracovian air). On the church facade itself are statues of Stanisław Kostka, Ignatius Loyola, Francis Xavier and Aloysius Gonzaga – all driving forces behind the Counter-Reformation. Above the entrance door is the Jesuit emblem whilst St Zygmunt and St Adalbert occupy the two niches at the top. The church was built between 1596 and 1619.

The interior is austere and surprisingly spacious, despite the fact that the nave is sandwiched between a number of chapels, rather than aisles. An information leaflet in English is available for a detailed appreciation of the various chapels. One must pay to enter the crypt; inside is the silver coffin of Piotr Skarga Pawęski - his enduring reputation is testified by the mass of thoughts, pleas and requests (usually written on the back of the entrance ticket) that lie on top of his tomb. You may choose to leave one there yourself.

Next door to the Church of Saints Peter and Paul is the eleventh century **Church of St Andrew** (*Kościół Św*

The maginificent facade of the church of Saints Peter and Paul

Andrzeja), considered to be the best surviving example of Romanesque architecture in the country. The heavy design of the church gives the place a very foreboding air, and indeed this is where many of Kraków's citizens sheltered during the Mongol rampages of 1241; the walls are some 1.6m (5ft) thick and the windows very narrow and placed high up. In marked contrast to the plain exterior of the church, the compact interior was decked out in a very florid late-baroque style in the eighteenth century; note in particular the exuberance of the pulpit constructed in the style of a boat (representing that of Saint Peter).

Along Grodzka to Wawel

Two more churches line Grodzka, though neither is likely to be open unless there is a service on. The **Church of St Martin** (*Kościół Św Marcina*) has its origins in the twelfth century, though it was given an early-baroque makeover; it was taken over by the Lutheran community in 1816. At the end of the street is the small **Church of St Giles** (*Kościół Św Idziego*), built in the fourteenth century on the site of a former Romanesque church. Many of the valuable interior furnishings date from the sixteenth and seventeenth centuries. At 10.30am every Sunday there is a service here in English. Next to the church is a cross which commemorates the 4500 Polish officers murdered by the Soviets in Katyń Forest in 1940 - a crime which the Soviet Union originally blamed on the Nazis when the mass grave was uncovered in 1943 (tellingly though, Katyń was removed from the list of Nazi war crimes at the Nuremberg trials).

Alternative: along Kanoniczna to Wawel

If you head back to St Mary Magdalene Square you can continue your tour up to Wawel Hill along Kanoniczna. At number 15 is a **Ukrainian Bookshop**, art gallery and restaurant housed in a medieval building known as the **Szreniawa House** (the Szreniawa family crest can be found on the facade).

The building at number 17 was once the bishop's palace and it originally dates from the fourteenth century; note the curious Gothic sloping window to the right of the doorway designed to allow more sunlight in. The next building along houses the city's **Archdiocesan Museum** (*Museum Archidiecezjalne*). It's a good, if hardly essential, collection of chalices, chasubles, paintings and the

Above: The city's Archaeological Museum is housed in a former prison complex

Below: The twin towers of the Church of St Andrew.

like and a fair portion of the exhibition is dedicated to the life of Pope John Paul II, a former Archbishop of Kraków; some of the photographs are interesting (it's rare to see pictures of him as a young man), though most astonishing to English eyes will be a symbolic painting of the Pontiff giving a two-fingered salute to the onlooker.

The corner house at the very end of Kanoniczna is known as **Długosz's House** after the fifteenth century Polish historian, soldier and diplomat who wrote the seminal twelve-volume *Historica Polonica* here. On the Podzamcze side of the building is a valuable seventeenth century wall painting of the Madonna and Child. You can still see the damage caused by 16 bullets, fired by marauding Russian troops in the eighteenth century.

Wawel

Though Rynek Główny may be the business centre of Kraków, Wawel is the spiritual heart of the city, and arguably of all Poland and a visit here is central to an understanding of the role that Kraków has played in the history of the Polish people.

Walk up the traditional route into Wawel which leads up from the end of Kanoniczna; until the nineteenth century this was the only route into the castle, though a road now winds around the back of the hill. The first gate you pass through is called the **Heraldic Gate** (*Brama Herbowa*), as it is adorned with coats of arms of the lands of the former Republic of Poland and Lithuania. To your right is the ticket office for the Royal Castle while to your left is a statue of Tadeusz Kościuszko, who led the unsuccessful 1794 National Uprising against the Russians - the suppression of the revolt led directly to the partition of Poland and its disappearance from the map of Europe. The second gate, the baroque **Vasa Gate** (*Brama Wazów*), lets you into the heart of the castle and to your immediate left stands the impressive cathedral doorway.

The Cathedral

This is the third cathedral to have been built on Wawel; the first was

The Royal Crypts

Władysław I Łokietek was the first Polish king to be buried in the cathedral back in 1333; after him nearly every Polish king was interned here, with a fair share too of queens and princes. The Royal Crypts were used from the mid-sixteenth century onwards; before this kings were buried in vaults under the floor of the cathedral - and their exact whereabouts are not all known.

The first room you enter after the vestibule is **St Leonard's Crypt**. The Romanesque round arches here tell you that this part of the building dates back to the eleventh century, and is part of the second version of the cathedral. The dim, solemn nature of the place contrasts markedly with the constant stream of chattering tourists flowing through it. The gold letters on the floor reveal that Bishop Maurus (the fourth successor of St Stanisław) was buried under there in 1118. The most recent addition to the room is General Władysław Sikorski (1881-1943) who led the Polish government in exile during the Nazi occupation (he's located immediately to your left as you enter). Explore the rest of the Royal Crypts at your leisure; all the coffins are labelled. The final crypt you enter contains the simple coffin of Marshal Józef Piłsudski (1867-1935), a hugely respected figure in Poland who is largely credited for the reconstitution of Poland at the end of World War I; it was he who proclaimed Polish independence in 1918 and who launched the military offensive against the Russians in 1919 which saw the reclamation of Polish territories to the east. Your tour will eventually lead you outside the cathedral from where you will have to return back via the main entrance.

built around 1000, the second was constructed in the late eleventh century and burned down in 1305, while this present Gothic construction was built between 1320 and 1364 and is officially termed the **Church of Saints Wenceslas and Stanisław** (*Katedra Św Wacława i Stanisława*). The ticket office is located opposite the entrance; you do not need a ticket to enter the cathedral but you do need one to visit the crypts and to see Zygmunt's Bell. Guides tend to congregate around the ticket office and, of all the places in the city, this is where you will probably appreciate one the most.

Walking up the entrance stairway you will notice to the left of the door some large **bones** chained to the wall. These once belonged to a whale, a rhinoceros and a mammoth, though legend relates they are the remains of an ancient giant who used to roam these parts. Local tradition states that should the chain break and the bones fall to the ground, it would be a sign that the end of the world is nigh.

Straight ahead of you as you enter the cathedral is the centrepiece of the complex, the bright silver **shrine of St Stanisław**, the patron saint of Poland. The shrine was built in 1626-9, though the original coffin was lost during the Swedish invasion of the 1650s and the present one dates to 1671; the reliefs on the side depict episodes from his life.

Walk around the shrine to the chancel to get a proper sense of the totality of the church, the most important in Poland, for this is where the Polish kings were crowned and buried. The main altar dates from the seventeenth century; the bishop's throne stands to the right while to the left is a memorial to Cardinal Adam Stefan Sapieha (1867-1951), former Archbishop of Kraków. In the middle of the stairs leading up to the altar is the tomb of Cardinal Fryderyk Jagiellończyk (1468-1503), one of thirteen children of King Kazimierz IV Jagiellończyk (four of his brothers were kings). Notice hanging above you the massive seventeenth century Dutch tapestries, adding a sense of grandeur but also some intimacy to the place.

Each side of the church is lined by a succession of **chapels** which provide not only an invaluable evocation of religious piety, but also a unique cross-section of architecture, painting and sculpture since the fourteenth century. Start the tour back at the entrance, along the northern aisle.

The first chapel to be seen is the **Holy Trinity Chapel**, or the Chapel of Queen Zofia after Queen Zofia Holszańska who endowed it. Zofia was the fourth and last wife of Władysław II Jagiełło and was Queen of Poland from 1422-61; as well as finally providing the king with a male heir (he was 71 when they wed), she also sponsored the translation of the Bible into Polish. The stained glass windows create a surprising kaleidoscope of colours which play very prettily with the gold and red of the interior decor - the result of an Art Nouveau retouch at the beginning of the twentieth century. Opposite the entrance, the lady with the fuller figure draped on the couch is aristocrat Konstancja Tyszkiewiczowa (d.1867), while to the right you can just about see Włodzimierz Potocki (1789-1812), a nobleman and officer, who is dressed

Top: The entrance to the Cathedral
Below: Wawel Hill, Castle and Cathedral

up as a Roman soldier (the sculpture was commissioned after his death by his wife, Tekla Sanguszkowna, who later married her valet).

The next chapel, the **Czartoryski Chapel**, forms the entranceway down to the **Royal Crypts** (*Krypty Królewskie*). Exiting the Royal Crypts leads you out of the cathedral which you must re-enter via the main doorway.

Just along and opposite the Czartoryski Chapel is the **effigy of King Władysław III Warneńczyk**, who died in 1444 at the tender age of twenty whilst fighting the Turks at the Battle of Varna (his body was never recovered); the piece dates to 1906 and is the work of Antoni Madeyski (1862-1939). The next chapel along is that of **Bishop Samuel Maciejowski** who died in 1550, though the altar is eighteenth century; the reason most Poles have to celebrate him is because he founded the popular spa resort of Krynica.

You will notice now the stairway leading down to the **Poets' Crypt** (*Krypta Wieszczów*) which contains the remains of two of Poland's finest romantic poets, Adam Mickiewicz (1798-1855) and Juliusz Słowacki (1809-49). Mickiewicz is probably best known for his epic poem *Pan Tadeusz*, which portrays an idyllic picture of village life in early nineteenth century Lithuania (it should be said that at the time he was writing the concept of Lithuania would have encompassed most of present day Poland, and indeed much of Belarus and the Ukraine). Although he wrote all his major works in Polish, Mickiewicz spent most of his life in France. He died of cholera in Constantinople while trying to organise a Polish legion to fight against the Russians in the Crimean War, and his remains were transported from France to Kraków in 1900. Like Mickiewicz, Słowacki spent most of his life outside his homeland; he was exiled for his part in the failed 1848 Wielkopolska Uprising against the Prussians. Originally buried in the Montmartre cemetery in Paris, his remains were brought here in 1927. A commemorative memorial by the exit draws attention to fellow romantic poet Cyprian Kamil Norwid (1821-83). Norwid's work was unappreciated during his lifetime - much of which was spent in poverty and ill-health - but he is now considered one of Poland's most important writers. In 2001 soil from the collective grave in Paris where he had been buried was sent to the cathedral to be enshrined in the crypt.

The sombre tones of the baroque **Lipski Chapel**, dedicated to St Matthew the Evangelist, contains a stunning memorial to Cardinal Jan Lipski (1690-1746) - who became King August III in 1733 - on its east wall.

The Zygmunt Bell

Steep wooden steps in the Zygmunt Tower take you up a disturbingly dark stairway to the huge ten-ton Zygmunt Bell (*Dzwon Zygmunt*), made in 1520 from gun barrels at the behest of King Zygmunt I. The weight of the clapper alone is an astonishing 300kg (660lb); it takes ten men to swing it and women who touch it are said to find fortune in matters of the heart. Because of its delicate state, the bell is only rung on the major church holidays but when it is, it's said to be heard up to 50km (30 miles) away. According to popular belief the noise is enough to drive the clouds away and bring sunshine. There are four other smaller bells in the tower, ranging in date from 1455 to 1751.

Also in the chapel is the tomb of Bishop Andrzej Lipski, who died in 1631 - he was Bishop of Kraków for just one year. Next along, the **Skotnicki family Chapel** features an interesting sculpture of an indolent woman seemingly examining her nails, actually a monument to the painter Michal Skotnicki (d.1808) - hence the brushes at her feet. Next along is **Bishop Zebrzydowski's Chapel**; he was Bishop of Kraków from 1551-60 and reputedly a fairly poor defender of the Catholic faith against the new Protestant heresies - a popular phrase often attributed to him is "you may believe in what you will, provided you pay me the tithe". A little along and opposite the chapel is the fourteenth century **tomb of King Władysław I**

Łokietek, the father of Kazimierz the Great (who commissioned the piece); this is the oldest royal sarcophagus in the cathedral, though the canopy was added only in 1903.

St Margaret's Chapel now serves as the entrance to the Cathedral Treasury, though this is presently closed to the general public (the most important parts of the collection are on display in the Cathedral Museum anyway). The chapel also gives entrance to the fourteenth century **Zygmunt Tower** (*Wieża Zygmuntowska*).

Back in the church, next to the entrance to the tower is a large crucifix known as the **Black Crucifix of Queen Jadwiga,** who ascended the Polish throne at the age of ten (and was crowned as King) in 1384; according to tradition she is said to have heard voices when praying here telling her to convert the Lithuanians (Europe's last pagans) and in 1386 she married the Grand Duke of Lithuania who had agreed to convert to the Catholic faith as a condition of the marriage - the two countries were to be linked for the next 400 years. Renowned for her numerous acts of charity and the foundation of several hospitals, Jadwiga was extremely popular with the populas at large and it is said that in 1399 the townspeople of Kraków beseiged the castle with gifts as she lay dying from the result of complications following the birth of her daughter (who also sadly passed away). In 1987 when Pope John Paul II visited the cathedral, he placed the relics of Queen Jadwiga in a chamber inside the altar, and in 1997 Jadwiga was canonised.

The **Chapel of Bishop Gamrat** is a fourteenth century construction housing the tomb of the former Bishop of Kraków, an unpopular religious zealot in his time. Behind the chancel is **St Mary's Chapel**, slightly too overwrought for most people's tastes though the busily decorated sixteenth century altar is worthy of attention; the chapel was at one time directly connected to the castle via a passageway. The **Chapel of Tomicki** contains a small silver coffin containing the relics of one of Poland's first chroniclers

The chakrah

According to some Hindus, Wawel Hill is one of seven holy places in the world linked to the presence of a mysterious source of divine energy contained in a stone called a **chakrah** (said to be found in the corner of the courtyard nearest to your left as you enter). The other places containing this stone are said to be Velehrad, Rome, Jerusalem, Delphi, Mecca and Delhi.

The chakrah energy is supposed to have a great effect on the people living around it, and that is why great civilizations have grown up around them - the energy is supposed to protect the city until the end of time. While this may at first hearing seem almost unbelievably fanciful it has been proved that there is indeed very strong natural radiation on Wawel, and so there may be some factual basis to the belief (note however that the Wawel authorities dismiss these claims utterly and official Wawel tour guides are not permitted to even mention the chakrah).

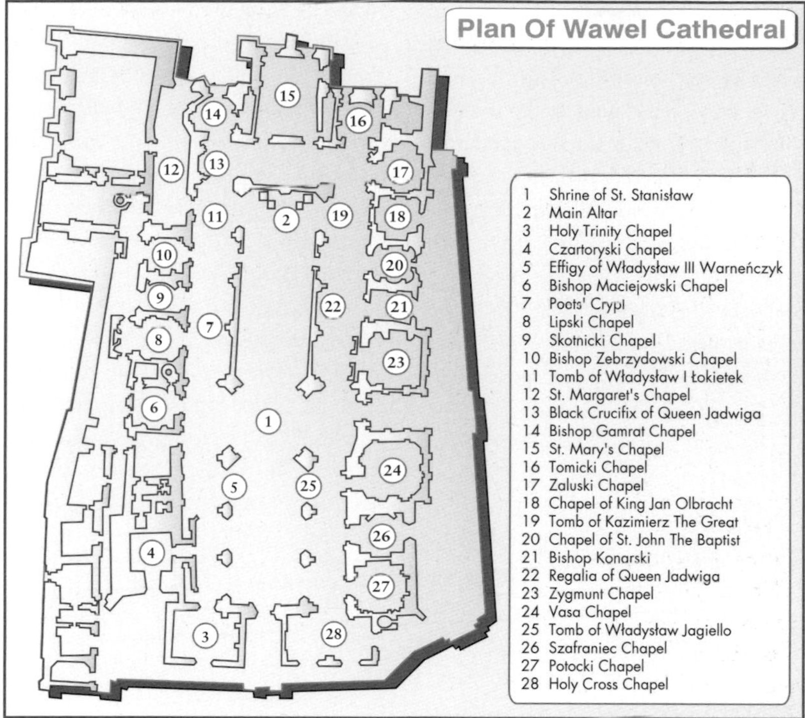

Wincenty Kadłubek (d.1223) - who was also Bishop of Kraków.The **Chapel of Andrzej Stanisław Załuski** dates originally from the fourteenth century; it was given a vibrant rococo rehash in the eighteenth century and the prissy looking bishop appears to be on the verge of dancing, while the two angels in the corner to your left at the base of the column look as if they're in the midst of the hokey-cokey. It was Załuski's brother who founded the first public library in Europe, in Warsaw in 1748 - it housed some 400,000 books but the collection was seized by the Russian army in 1795 and it has never been recovered.

Next along is the **Chapel of King Jan Olbracht**. Here rests the said king (responsible for the building of the Barbican by the Floriańska gate) and it has to be said that he looks supremely restful - look very carefully and you might even see his chest moving up and down! Opposite the chapel is the **tomb of Kazimierz the Great** **(see box p.9)** which dates from the fourteenth century.The **Chapel of St John the Baptist** (also known as the Chapel of Bishop Zadzik) used to serve as the royal dressing room before coronations. The tiny **Chapel of Bishop Konarski** dates to 1351 but underwent many facelifts before finally settling on a baroque style in the early eighteenth century; pastel hues dominate in the stained glass window.

Opposite the Konarski chapel is a reliquary with the **regalia of Queen Jadwiga**, who we've already met; the very worn-looking wooden orb and sceptre were once gilded with gold. Their existence came to light in 1949 when they were found in the queen's tomb. Next along is her **sarcophagus**, a surprisingly recent work by Antoni Madeyski dating only from 1902; her feet rest on a sleeping dog, which symbolises fidelity. Jadwiga's tomb used to be by the main altar, in 1949 her remains were placed here where they remained until they were transferred to the Black Crucifix in 1987.

The most famous of the cathedral's chapels is the **Zygmunt Chapel** (*Kaplica Zygmuntowska*), also known as the Royal Chapel. This is the glorious copper-domed chapel that you can see outside (it's regularly re-roofed to keep the sheen). It was built between 1519 and 1531 by the Florentine Bartolomeo Berrecci (1480-1537) and is considered to be one of the highlights of Renaissance style this side of the Alps. The chapel is an original work, not based on any pre-existing Italian structure, though the influence of Roman triumphal arches on the architecture of the chapel is obvious, and the dome echoes that of the cathedral in Florence. The precise meaning of the plainly mythological and classical decoration (Hercules and Cleopatra make an appearance, as do various sea monsters and even some naked nymphs) has puzzled art historians for years; it probably represents some kind of attempt to reconcile classical learning with Christian tradition. To the right are two tombs; King Zygmunt I (r.1506-48) lies on top of his son King Zygmunt August (r.1548-72) and the figures both look as if they've just fallen asleep on a sofa - very much a Renaissance stylisation.

Wawel Cathedral

Next along is the **Vasa Chapel**, built in the mid-seventeenth century using the Zygmunt Chapel as its blueprint, though the two chapels leave vastly different impressions. This one being much more sombre and gloomy, almost overwhelmed with death. Indeed, it's almost completely black.

Just opposite the Vasa Chapel is the red marble **tomb of King Władysław Jagiełło** (r.1386-1434) who was the Lithuanian husband of Queen Jadwiga; he founded the bishopric of Vilnius and organised mass baptisms of his people immediately after the marriage. The dragon at his feet adds a suitable pagan touch (it's supposed to symbolize the king's triumph over evil, while the two lions under his head represent his power). The tomb was probably made during his lifetime, though the canopy dates from 1524. The next chapel along is the vehemently red baroque

Szafraniec Chapel dedicated to St Stephen; the stained glass window is a relatively recent 1908 addition.

The light and airy interior of the **Potocki Chapel** acts as a nice contrast; originally founded in 1381, it was reconditioned in 1840 in neo-classical style. The final chapel is the **Holy Cross Chapel** dating to 1447-92 and late Gothic in style. King Kazimierz Jagiellończyk (r.1447-92), a towering figure in late-fifteenth century Europe whose domains stretched from the Baltic to the Adriatic and from Prague to Kursk, is buried here in a red marble tomb to your left - a plaque on the floor on the other side of the chapel marks the final resting place of his wife, Queen Elżbieta. Directly in front of you is the **tomb of Bishop Kajetan Sołtyk** which dates from 1788, a classical intrusion in the late Gothic menagerie.

Above: Old Cannons in the castle grounds

Top: The castle courtyard

The Cathedral Museum *(Muzeum Katedralne)*

The museum was founded in 1978 and is housed in buildings which used to serve as the servants' quarters. Most of the collection comes from the Cathedral Treasury; highlights include a remarkable chasuble (an ornate overgown used by a priest during mass) dating from 1504 which features a 3-dimensional relief in fabric depicting scenes from the legend of St Stanisław, several robes belonging to John Paul II, and, slightly bizarrely, a cross that Edwin (Buzz) Aldrin took to the moon.

The Royal Chambers

What follows is a description of the entire Royal Chambers complex. These are explored on two separate tours; one taking you around the State Rooms and the other around the Royal Apartments. Each room has an internal map in English, which explains fully what is on display and where the items are from, though generally the interiors tend to be quite bare, evoking not so much a glorious past as a sense of what has been lost over the centuries.

The State Rooms

The first room you enter (prosaically named Governor's Apartment – Room 1) is notable for its three seventeenth-century tapestries, which depict *Achilles with Agamemnon, Priam welcoming Helen, and The History of Celadon and Astrea.* The next room along houses a much worn sixteenth-century Flemish tapestry featuring the god Mars (the four poster bed is of English origin and dates from the sixteenth century). The room adjoining boasts a number of interesting Polish money chests. From here you enter another chamber featuring yet more chests and a staircase. At the top of the staircase is a hallway leading up to the first and second floors (on the first floor are the Royal Apartments which are accessed on a separate tour). Most impressive in the hallway itself is the huge and vivid seventeenth-century tapestry from Brussels depicting a stag hunt.

On the second floor, you enter first the **Tournament Room** which takes its title from the tournament frieze painted in the early sixteenth century by Antoni of Wroclaw and Hans Dürer (brother of Albrecht). Also on display is a very colourful eighteenth-century stove from Wisniowiec Castle. The next room is called the **Hall of the Military Review** and is named after another frieze by Antoni of Wroclaw, painted in 1535 (the king depicted is King Sigismund I). More impressive here though are the five tapestries, all dating from around 1560.

One of the most important rooms in the complex is the **Audience Hall**, which is also one of the largest. The frieze around the wall depicts man's journey from birth to inevitable death while the tapestries contain depictions of various flora and fauna as well as one of God speaking to Noah. However, the throne here is not the real throne but rather a grand armchair dating from the sixteenth century. Look above you at the ceiling to see the most bizarre aspect of the decor, the so-called **Wawel Heads** dating from the sixteenth century, which peer down at you with generally moronic, if entertaining, expressions. Only 30 of the original 194 heads survive and it is not known exactly what they were made for or meant to depict (probably an illustration of some story or chronicle). According to popular legend, one of the heads actually started speaking during a trial that was taking place in the room, declaring the innocence of a woman who had been accused of stealing. Although the woman was acquitted it was decided that the head should not be allowed to interfere with any more judgments, and so a wooden gag was added to its mouth, which can be seen today.

Return to the hallway and then walk across to the **Zodiac Room**, which used to function as the main castle dining room. The frieze has an obvious astrological theme and the massive tapestry depicts the *Building of the Tower of Babel*. The frieze in the **Planets Room** is of (predictably) the planets and is a 1929 work by Leonard Pekalski which uses the same subject matter as the room's lost original; the tapestry here depicts God blessing Noah. The frieze in the next room once again gives the room its name – the **Battle of Orsza Room**; the battle took place in 1514; again this is a modern-day version by Pekalski. The **Bird Room** is interesting in so much as the walls are covered with bright red and yellow cordovan (leather), a type of wallpaper. The subsequent rooms in the tour also have this feature as does the small chapel that abuts the Bird Room.

The following vestibule was King Sigismund III's dining room during the late sixteenth century; a picture of him on horseback adorns the wall. The **Eagle Room** takes its name from a carved eagle which was once in the middle of the ceiling; this has been replaced by an allegorical painting depicting the rebirth of Poland, dating to 1933. The next vestibule leads to the **Senators' Hall**, the largest room, where senate meetings, artistic performances and balls would have taken place. During the Nazi era the room was transformed into a cinema. The story of Adam and Eve is depicted on the five tapestries here.

The Royal Apartments

The **Royal Apartments** are entered via the hallway on the first floor of the castle. The first room features several tapestries depicting various animals, as well as some valuable sixteenth-century paintings, including one by Lucas Cranach (the furniture is Italian and dates to the sixteenth century). Seven more tapestries decorate the next room along, while the third room has a number of valuable paintings as well as a colourful Baroque stove (the furniture is again Italian). The fourth room features a four-poster bed from England (seventeenth century) and also boasts the oldest surviving tapestry in Wawel – it depicts a knight with a swan and dates from around 1460.

Walk now back through these four rooms and across the hallway to continue the tour. The first two rooms you enter are normally used to house various temporary exhibitions. Following these is a vestibule that leads to a series of rooms comprising the most intimate area of the castle, the private quarters of the royal family; most interesting is the tiny **Hen's Foot Tower** which projects outside the main walls, originally fourteenth-century Gothic in design though given a baroque makeover in the seventeenth century.

The Courtyard

Walk now into the centre of the castle. The courtyard was filled with residential dwellings until the early nineteenth century when they were demolished by the Austrians to create a parade ground. To your left is the Royal Castle itself; turning clockwise, the **Lost Wawel Exhibition** is housed by the refreshments bar. On the grass (which you can't walk on) are the foundations of two medieval churches and the house of Canon Jan Borek - none particularly photogenic. To your right is the old hospital building (where the main ticket office for the castle is), which stands between the Sandomierz Tower to the left and the Thieves' Tower (where, as the name suggests, thieves were once incarcerated) to the right; both these towers date to the early sixteenth century. The road out of the castle here takes you past the entrance to the **Dragon's Cave** (see p.72).

Into the Royal Castle *(Zamek Królewski)*

The tour of the Royal Castle interior comprises four exhibitions: the State Rooms, the Royal Apartments, the Oriental Art exhibition and the Treasury and Armoury. Of the four, the Royal Chambers and State Rooms are the more essential viewing if time is limited. There are two ticket offices, one in the old hospital building, the other just before the Vasa Gate. The ticket to the State Rooms and Royal Apartments will have an entrance time printed on it as the exhibitions get so busy (particularly in summer and at weekends) that only a limited number of visitors are let in at any one time. To avoid standing in the queue you can call the box office on 422 1697 and reserve tickets in advance (pick them up at the Tourist Service Office on Wawel Hill on the day). The Royal Apartments may only be visited on a guided tour - tours in English run quite regularly, ask when you buy your ticket. You must leave any bags at the designated luggage rooms before entering any of the exhibitions.

The first building on this spot was a Romanesque palace which was replaced by a Gothic castle in the fourteenth century and then, in the sixteenth century, by the present Renaissance construction built by King Zygmunt I. Its days of glory essentially ended in 1609 when Zygmunt II left Kraków to march on Moscow; upon his return to Poland he set up his court in Warsaw, and Wawel was subsequently used only for royal coronations and funerals.

The castle was sacked by the Swedes in 1655, and in 1702 a major fire damaged much of the interior. Only in the late nineteenth century was the place restored to anything like its former glory; and after independence in 1918 a concerted, and partially successful, attempt was made to repatriate some of the old furnishings. During the Second World War the Nazis took over the castle, and it became the headquarters of the local governor general Hans Frank.

On initial viewing, the inner courtyard may seem disappointingly plain, but the arcaded galleries produce a graceful, if slightly austere, effect, and the sixteenth century wall paintings you can see to your upper right as you enter give some idea of the majesty of decoration once here - the roof would at one time have been covered with multi-coloured tiles woven in intricate patterns, and the courtyard floor covered with red brick.

The Treasury and Armoury

What you see today in the **Treasury** (*Skarbiec Koronny*) represents only a small fraction of a collection repeatedly plundered over the centuries. Pride of place amongst the exhibits stands the thirteenth century sword used for the coronation of Polish kings. Also of priceless value are the crown of King Zygmunt I, the oldest surviving royal banner (1533) and King Kazimierz the Great's fourteenth century chalice. Various medals, jugs and basins of varying degrees of interest make up the rest of the display, most of which is labelled in English.

The **Armoury** (*Zbrojownia*) features highlights from five centuries of warfare (various guns, cannons, swords, crossbows and banners). Perhaps most interesting is the collection of armour; particularly impressive is the late seventeenth century *karacena* (scale) armour, almost fish-like in appearance. Not many people linger in the armoury, but on a hot summer's day at least it's cool inside (and, conversely, it's a relatively warm place to be in winter).

The Oriental Exhibition *(Sztuka Wschodu)*

The Oriental Exhibition is essentially a collection of oriental booty captured during the wars against the Turks. The most precious exhibits are the fine Persian carpets, though there are also collections of pottery, armour and weapons on show.

The Wawel Tapestries

The Wawel tapestries are the castle's greatest treasure. The oldest were woven in Arras, France during the fourteenth and fifteenth centuries, and came to Poland as part of the dowry of Bona Sforza, wife of King Sigismund I. He was so impressed that he immediately bought some more from Antwerp. The collection was then enhanced by King Sigismund Augustus who ordered a series of works from Brussels in the years 1550-71, specifying minutely the size, subject matter and materials to be used (only the finest, of course). This took the total number of tapestries in Wawel up to 360.

Only 136 survive today – and we are lucky there is even that number. When King Jan Casimir (1648-60) abdicated, he took part of the collection to France and left the rest with a pawnbroker in Gdańsk. The Polish parliament did not recover the Gda sk portion until the eighteenth century, though they were appropriated by Russians in 1795, with whom they stayed until finally returned to Wawel in 1921. They went travelling once again to escape the clutches of the Nazis – to Romania, then France, England and Canada – before a final return to the castle in 1961.

The Legend of the Dragon's Cave

According to popular tradition a fearsome dragon lived in this cave at the time of legendary King Krak, who apparently offered half his kingdom and his daughter's hand in marriage to anyone who could slay the terrible thing. Many a brave and ambitious knight was either eaten or scared off until a humble cobbler had the bright idea of leaving a lamb's skin filled with sulphur by the entrance to the cave. When the dragon ate it the sulphur burned its insides; the monster drank so heavily from the river to quench its thirst that its stomach burst open and it died.

The Lost Wawel Exhibition *(Wawel Zaginiony)*

This is located next to the refreshments bar. A small cinema near the entrance shows a virtual reality film of the history of Wawel, while the exhibition itself is primarily a walk over some of the excavations of the site; the most important being the **Rotunda of the Virgin**, built around the tenth century as a palace chapel, and thus one of Poland's first Christian churches. Also to be seen are remains of a palace and a skeleton found during the diggings.

The Dragon's Cave *(Smocza Jama)*

Now exit Wawel across the courtyard, the way to the so-called Dragon's Cave.

This is one of many limestone caves in Wawel Hill which have served different functions over the centuries from sheltering the homeless to storing fish even to housing taverns and whorehouses - King Henry de Valois is said to have been a regular at the Dragon's Cave brothel in the sixteenth century. This is the only cave you can enter today, and it's a one way system; the entrance is on the top of the Wawel Hill and the exit by the River Wisła. By the exit is a fire breathing (in summer) bronze statue of the dragon, and very frightening it is too!

From here you can walk along Bernardyńska, a good place to get photographs of Wawel as a whole. Here you will also find the Church of St Bernard, which is where chapter three begins.

Places to visit in Wawel

Archaeological Museum

Poselska 3

Open: Mon to Wed 9am-2pm; Thu 2–6pm; Fri 10am–2pm; Sun 10am–2pm.

Centre for the Documentation of the Art of Tadeusz Kantor

Cricot 2 Theatre

Kanoniczna 5

Open: Mon–Fri 10am-2pm, July and Aug only

Geological Museum

Senacka

Open: Thu and Fri 10am–3pm; Sat 10am–2pm

Archdiocesan Museum

Kanoniczna 19

Open: Tue–Fri 10am–4pm; Sat and Sun 10am–3pm

Wawel

Cathedral

Open: Mon–Sat 9am–5.30pm (3pm in Winter); Sun and holidays 2.15–5:30pm

Cathedral Museum

Open: Tue-Sun 10am–3pm

Treasury and Armoury

Open: Tue-Sat 9:30am–4pm; Sun 10am–4pm

Royal Chambers

Open: Tue-Sun 9:30am–4pm

State Rooms

Open: Tue–Sat 9:30am–4pm; Sun 10am–4pm

Oriental Exhibition

Open: Tue–Sat 9.30am–4pm

Lost Wawel Exhibition

Open: Wed–Sun 9:30am–3pm

Dragon's Cave

Open: daily 10am–5pm. Closed 31 Oct–31 March

3. Stradom, Kazimierz and Podgórze

From its founding in 1335 until 1800 **Kazimierz,** the area to the south-east of Wawel, was a separate settlement from Kraków, incorporating Jewish and Christian quarters; **Stradom** grew up along the road linking it with Wawel. Nowadays both areas lie outside the very centre of the city, close enough to the Rynek Główny and the Castle to still be popular with tourists but far enough away to give the area a special, quieter character compared to the centre of town.

Left: Oscar Schindler's factory - its exterior still as it looked in the 1940s and as used in the filming of Schindler's List

Opposite page:: The Missionary Church of St Paul

Although Stradom boasts a couple of interesting sites, and the Christian part of Kazimierz is home to two magnificent and historically important churches, it's the Jewish quarter of Kazimierz which is the real draw in this part of town: no other part of Kraków bears the weight of twentieth century history as much as this area does. Once it was the focal point for Kraków's huge Jewish population. Now, after decades of neglect following the catastrophe of World War Two, it's once more vibrant, with busy restaurants and restored synagogues jostling for attention among the austere, grey streets and courtyards. Even if you are pressed for time and don't take a look around this area, you should at least head for one of the Jewish-style restaurants on Szeroka (pp.144-45), which have a warm, refined air that reflects the uniqueness of this part of the city. A short distance away from these restaurants, with their traditional Jewish music and food, is a part of the city little visited by tourists, which carries reminders of some of the darkest times in Kraków's history - when the area of **Podgórze** formed a Jewish ghetto prior to the destruction of the Jewish community in 1943.

Stradom

The area immediately south of Wawel is traditionally known as Stradom; a settlement grew up here in the Middle Ages on the road (*Stradomska*) that leads between Kraków and Kazimierz. In the early fifteenth century Stradom was amalgamated with the settlement of Kazimierz which was separated from it by a branch of the Wisła River that ran along present-day Józefa Dietla Street.

Begin the walk at the baroque **Church of St Bernard** (*Kościół Bernardynów*) which dates from the late seventeenth century (although there has been a church on this site since 1453); the square in front was used for church fairs. The busy interior is slightly gloomy, however it does boast some very valuable paintings - look out for the depiction of the Danse Macabre in the Chapel of St Anne in the left aisle, which also houses a wooden statue of said saint sculpted in the Veit Stoss workshop in the early sixteenth century. Another chapel contains the relics of St Syzmon of Lipnica, a pious Bernardine monk, who died in 1482.

A short walk down Stradomska (derived from *la strada*, the Italian for road) takes you to the **Missionary Church of St Paul** (*Kościół Misjonarzy*), an early eighteenth-century baroque building designed by a former mayor of Kraków, Kasper Bazanka. The interior is quiet and relatively unprepossessing but a series of colourful paintings on the ceiling brighten up the place considerably.

Follow Stradomska to the major junction with Józefa Dietla, laid in 1880, which follows the old river bed of the Wisła.

Krakówska and Plac Wolnica

Beyond this crossroads is the district of Kazimierz and Stradomska becomes known as Krakówska; this was old Kazimierz's main thoroughfare which divided Christian and Jewish quarters. Most of the buildings along Krakówska date back at least as far as the nineteenth century. Follow the street south to plac Wolnica, Kazimierz's old market place, which is dominated by the city's **Ethnographic Museum** (*Muzeum Etnograficzne*). In the Middle Ages plac Wolnica would have been some four times larger - almost equalling the size of Rynek Glówny, the main Kraków square - but during the nineteenth century the incursion of buildings severely limited its size. On the square is an interesting modern fountain called the *Three Street Musicians*.

Ethnographic Museum

This huge museum is housed in Kazimierz's former town hall. The town hall existed on this spot at the town's foundation, though the building's present day appearance dates to 1623; the city's collection of folk art was transferred here in 1949. It's a surprisingly good museum as well (with some friendly staff), well worth the paltry entrance fee to look around. The ground floor is the most interesting: a succession of reconstructed interiors of traditional houses. Upstairs are collections of painted Easter eggs, Christmas cribs (*szopki*), clothes and the like.

Further down Krakówska is the Baroque **Bonifrater Church of the Holy Trinity** (*Kościół Bonifratów*), built in the late eighteenth century by the Trinitarians, whose principal function was to pay the ransom of prisoners. Inside, on the ceiling, you can see a depiction of the order's founder, John of Matha, giving money for the release of prisoners from the Turks.

Back at the north-eastern corner of plac Wolnica is the Gothic brick **Corpus Christi Church** (*Kościół Bożego Ciała*). This hugely impressive construction was founded in 1340 and completed in 1405, and was the first church built in Kazimierz. It is said to have been built on the spot where the monstrance stolen from the All Saints Church was found discarded - today it is in the sacristy and it is said to offer the church protection.

Although the exterior is Gothic, the inside had a baroque makeover. The brick interior gives the place a slightly cold feeling - it feels as if you're on the outside of a building - but there are a number of interesting features; pay particular attention to the beautiful stalls in the chancel which date from the seventeenth century. The large altarpiece boasts two wonderful paintings (said to be the work of Tomaso Dolabella) and dates from 1637 while, slightly strangely, the pulpit is in the shape of a boat, a reference to Peter who used to preach to the masses from his. The church also contains the supposedly miracle-inducing relics of Stanisław Kazimierczyk (d.1489) in its northern aisle (they are kept in the small coffin); eleven pictures here tell the story of his life.

A short walk away on św Wawrzyńca, located in the old tram depot, is the **Museum of Municipal Engineering** (*Muzeum Inżynierii Miejskiej*), basically a collection of cars and motorcycles manufactured in Poland since the 1930s, together with a couple of municipal trams. Adjoining is an exhibitions room - the exhibition changes but it is usually orientated towards children, with a hands-on approach to educate in matters of science and technology (in summer there is an outdoor playground). The museum forms part of what is called The Kraków Industrial Heritage Route which takes in various factories, bridges, power stations and the like - a free booklet is available at the ticket office for anybody particularly interested. The tram depot directly across the street now houses a go-kart track.

Jewish Kazimierz

In the early 1990s Jewish Kazimierz was a place that very few people visited; virtually the whole area around Szeroka was in a dilapidated state and the lack of street lighting made any venture here a thoroughly unnerving experience. However, things have changed to a major degree (and largely due to the attention that the area has received following the success of *Schindler's List*); synagogues have been restored, numerous smart hotels and restaurants have sprung up and the area has taken on an almost bohemian air with numerous bars, cafes, bookshops and art galleries opening

From the Corpus Christi Church walk down the street Józefa - formerly known as Zydowska, or Jewish Street, but renamed in honour of Emperor Joseph II who stayed in the house on the corner of Józefa and Krakówska (called Voivode's Mansion) during a visit in 1773. Eventually you will come to a small square faced by the **High Synagogue** (*Bożnica Wysoka*), once one of Kraków's most opulent, which was constructed in the mid-sixteenth century. The prayer hall was located on the first floor for security reasons; only fragments of the original wall decoration survived the Nazi desecration and today it houses a poignant exhibition of photographs taken of ordinary Jewish people in Kraków during the 1930s. The ground floor of the building presently houses a bookshop.

Szeroka, heart of Jewish Kraków

From here follow the road that leads to the main 'square' **Ulica Szeroka** or Broad Street, which has been the heart of Jewish Kraków since the sixteenth century. The most important building on Szeroka is the **Old Synagogue** (*Stara Synagoga*) at its southern end - originally built in the fifteenth centry, it burned down during the Great Fire of 1557 and was re-built in Renaissance style in the late sixteenth century. The building suffered more damage during fires in the sixteenth and seventeenth centuries and was restored at the beginning of the twentieth century. During the Second World War the Nazis completely ransacked the place; it was restored in the 1950s and the Museum of Judaism installed inside, but in spite of all the effort the interior today feels a little sterile. Arguably the most interesting things on display here are the photographs of old Kazimierz which

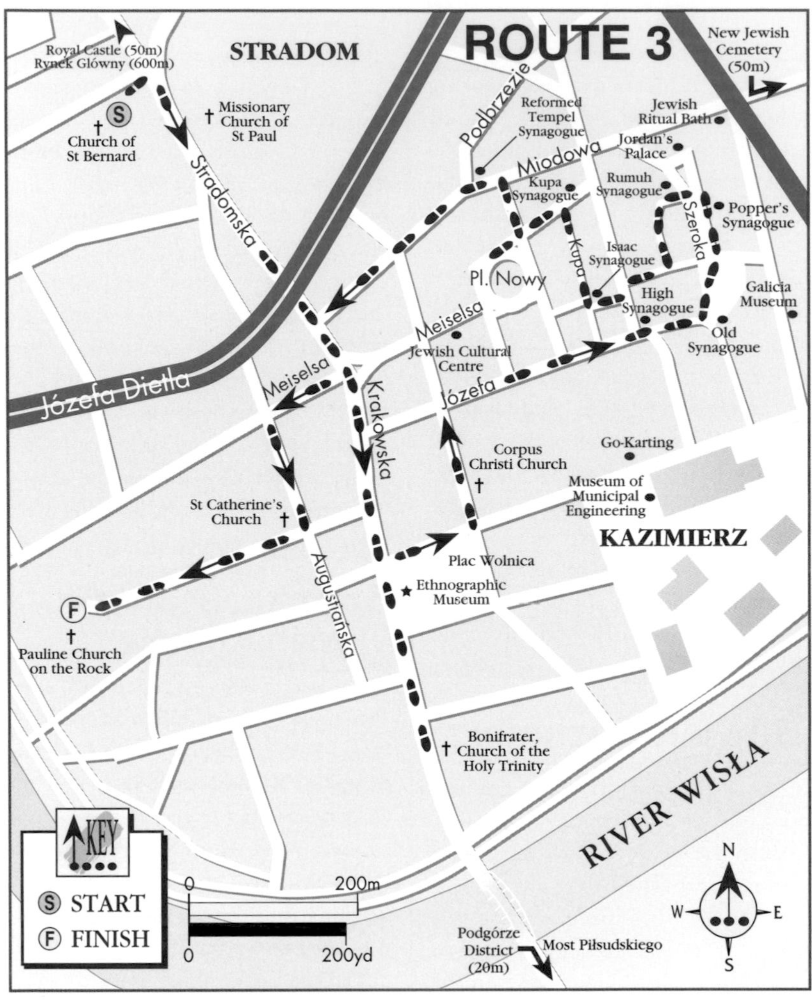

show a bustling street life long since departed. A hall adjoining the main prayer hall houses various temporary exhibitions, usually with an emphasis on the events of the war.

At the northern end of Szeroka is a small fenced area which was the original Jewish cemetery. Nearby is the **Rumuh Synagogue** which is the only synagogue in the city where services are still held (although it is often difficult to get enough people to turn up here for a service). Men will have to cover their heads upon entering - skullcaps are provided by the elderly gentlemen who sell tickets in the foyer. A wooden synagogue was originally built here in 1553, it burned down four years later in a fire that destroyed much of Kazimierz and then a new one was built which was renovated as you see it today in the early-nineteenth century. The interior was destroyed during the Second World War, when it was used by the Germans as a storage room, and restored in 1957. The fact that services still take place in this synagogue make it a different proposition from the Old Synagogue - less of a museum piece and much more evocative of the Jewish community that once lived in Kazimierz. The black plate on the wall commemorates those who have aided the restoration of the synagogue or contributed to its life in some way.

The **cemetery** behind the synagogue was originally founded in 1552 when some 200 plague victims were buried here. Its last burial was back at the end of the eighteenth century - the Austrians closed it for reasons of sanitation, and indeed it's very rare to find a cemetery located right in the heart of a Jewish town. The valuable Renaissance tombstones were buried by the Jews themselves to avoid desecration and by the beginning of the twentieth century the cemetery had become messily overgrown. Some minor restoration work took place before the war, but the place was predictably destroyed by the Nazis, who turned it into a rubbish tip.

Work began to thoroughly restore the cemetery in 1959 when hundreds of the fine collection of Renaissance tombstones were unearthed. As it was not known exactly who was buried where, the re-erected tombstones do not mark the burial place of the the person named on it. An exception to this, and the most valuable tomb here, belongs to the scholar and great codifier of Jewish law Rabbi Moses Isserles (1520-72), son of the merchant Israel Isserles who founded the Rumuh Synagogue in the sixteenth century. His tomb has become a sight of veneration for Jews who leave stones on top as a mark of respect, this is a custom which is said to derive from the time that the Jews spent in the desert when a pile of stones would mark a burial place. Many Jews from all over the world come here to pay their respects on the anniversary of his death, the Jewish holiday *Lag ba-Omer* (the exact date of which changes every year).

Above: The entrance to the Ethnographic Museum, which is housed in the old Kazimierz Town Hall

Almost directly opposite the Rumuh Synagogue, beyond the gate at number 16, is the **Popper's Synagogue** (*Bożnica Poppera*), built in 1620 by a wealthy merchant called Wolf Popper who had the habit of standing on one leg while he meditated (hence the building's alternative name, the Stork's Synagogue). The interior furnishings were destroyed during the Second World War but the building was reno-

The Legend of the Jewish Cemetery

An old Kraków legend tells of a wedding that took place in the Rumuh Cemetery back in medieval times, when plague was ravaging the country. According to tradition, one way of causing the plague to abate was to marry two old cripples in the Jewish cemetery, with the expenses being paid for by the community as a whole. And so, one Friday, a suitable blind hunchback was found in the poorhouse and married to a lame cleaning woman.

Drink flowed and the guests enjoyed themselves so much that they soon forgot the misery of the plague - and indeed the time! For the celebrations spilled over onto the Sabbath, a sin for which they were grievously punished: the ground underneath suddenly opened up, swallowing all of the revellers. It was a very strange occurrence, and since that time it has been forbidden to hold weddings in Kraków on a Friday.

vated in 1965 and it is now used to house various artistic exhibitions - it also puts on occasional theatrical and musical events.

The rest of this side of the square is taken up with a number of good restaurants and cafes, useful places to take a well-earned rest with a glass of beer (see pp144-45 for descriptions of the *Alef* and *Ariel* restaurants). In the evenings busloads of tourists are wheeled into the restaurants for recitals of Yiddish folk music; a kitsch experience undoubtedly, but as the beer flows, disbelief is suspended, and peering into the dimly lit interiors can be quite evocative. Note however that these are "Jewish-style" restaurants and are not kosher - Kraków's Jewish community being so small that no kosher food is prepared here - the only place where you can eat genuine kosher food in Kraków is at the *Eden Hotel* on Ciemna (advance warning required).

Flanking the northern side of Szeroka is the **Jordan's Palace** (*Pałac Jordanów*) (also known as the Landau Mansion), built in the sixteenth century by Spytko Jordan of Melsztyn and today occupied by a combined restaurant and bookshop. This is the best place to find books on the history of the Jews in Kraków and Poland in English, and they also organize walking tours of Jewish Kazimierz and bus tours to Auschwitz.

The hotel which stands on the north-eastern corner of Szeroka (the *Klezmer Hois,* see p.128) formerly housed a Jewish ritual bath or *mikveh* which functioned up to the beginning of the war. From here it is a short detour eastwards to the **New Jewish Cemetery** (*Nowy Cmentarz Żydowski*); simply follow the road Miodowa for 100m across Starowislna and under the railway bridge. This was founded in 1801 as the successor to the Rumuh Cemetery and is one of the few Jewish cemeteries in Poland which is still open (remember to keep your head covered when walking around here). It's much larger than the one on Szeroka, though it doesn't tend to be looked after quite as well. During the Second World War the Nazis turned the place into a recreation ground; it was reconstructed in the 1960s.

A short detour away from Szeroka at Dajwór 15 is the **Galicia Museum**. This houses an exhibition of modern photographs of Jewish buildings in the region (most in a dilapidated state or used for non-religious purposes).There is also a very good bookshop and cafe attached.

Szeroka to Miodowa

Back in the heart of Jewish Kazimierz, just west of Szeroka on Kupa, is the early Baroque **Isaac Synagogue** (*Synagoga Izaaka*), built in the mid-seventeenth century on behalf of a wealthy local merchant named Isaac Jakubowicz. Desecrated during the war, the building functioned as a sculptor's workshop and then a warehouse before being completely abandoned; it has been restored in phases since 1983 and was opened to the public in 1997.

Today the synagogue is at the forefront of the renaissance of Jewish culture in the city, with concerts, meetings and exhibitions taking place regularly; a special tourist information office has even been installed here. Every day in the main hall itself two films are continuously shown, each six minutes long: one is a random depiction of Jewish life in Kraków in 1936 (with the Isaac Synagogue itself in prominent shot), the other was taken by the Nazis and depicts the evacuation of the Jews from Kazimierz to the Podgórze ghetto south of the Wisła. In an annex there is an exhibition of stills from these and other films.

The **Kupa Synagogue** at Jonatana Warszauera 8 is a seventeenth-century construction which has undergone a number of major facelifts in the intervening period. None of the furnishings survived the Nazi destruction, though traces of paintings still remain on the old wooden ceiling. However, the building is presently not open to the general public.

The Legend of Isaac's Fortune

An interesting legend tells how the merchant Isaac Jakubowicz made his fortune. One night Isaac had a mysterious dream telling him to go to Prague where, upon a bridge across the Wisła, he would be given some good news. Isaac was a poor man and Prague a long way away, so he delayed his journey until the dream twice reoccurred and he felt obliged.

He reached the city, found the bridge and for seven days walked along it, hearing nothing. Then, just when he had decided to go back home, someone came up to him and asked him why he was spending so much time on the bridge. Isaac told him of his dream and the man laughed saying he'd had a similar one telling him of some treasure buried under a tree in the garden of a Jew named Isaac, who lived in Kraków. The man had never thought to venture to Kraków merely on the basis of a dream, especially as Isaac was such common Jewish name. The two men shook hands and Isaac eagerly went back home. Digging in his garden under the old pear tree he founded a chest filled to the brim with gold and jewellery. He used his money well, not only to help the poor but to also found the synagogue you see today.

Above: The Isaac Synagogue, a Baroque structure dating from the 1640s

Left: The High Synagogue, built in the Sixteenth century and devastated by the Nazis

In the middle of **plac Nowy** is a remarkable round building dating from 1900 which was built as a trade hall and from 1927-39 functioned as the Jewish ritual slaughterhouse. It's now a covered market and the shuttered windows are still used to serve customers. Everyday you will see a small number of stalls with local people selling their home-grown produce here - perhaps of more interest though is the antiques fair and flea market held every Saturday.

At Meiselsa 17, housed in a former prayer house, is a **Jewish Cultural Centre** which opened in 1993. The centre includes a cafe and library and they hold various temporary art exhibitions here as well as organising cultural events and showing films; it's best to simply walk in and have a look what's on.

The **Reformed (Tempel) Synagogue** (*Synagoga Tempel*) stands on Miodowa where it meets Podbrzezie. This was built in 1860-2 in Neo-Renaissance style. The "reformed" refers to the fact that services took place here in Polish and German, which is not the custom in an orthodox synagogue. It's the most modern looking of Kraków's synagogues, and in many ways the most impressive building in the quarter with a grand red and gold interior reminiscent of a nineteenth century London theatre - indeed, the venue is often used for concerts.

The Reformed Tempel Synagogue, a 19th century neo-Renaissance structure

Christian Kazimierz

Two magnificent churches stand in the western, and traditionally Christian, half of the Kazimierz district. A visit to them will round off your tour of the Jewish quarter and lead you back to the heart of the city.

St Catherine's Church (*Kościół Św Katarzyny*), on Augustiańska, used to stand on the corner of the main square in Kazimierz, which is a good indication of just how big it was. The church was founded in 1363 by King Kazimierz the Great to atone for the murder of a priest called Marcin Baryczka. The Bishop of Kraków had sent the unfortunate prelate with a message condemning the king for his exuberant love life, Kazimierz took such umbrage at this rebuke that he had Marcin put in a sack and submerged beneath the ice of the Wisła.

The church was twice severely damaged by earthquakes (firstly in 1443 and then again in 1786) after which it was used as a storehouse - it was not finally restored to its former glory until the nineteenth century. The church forms part of an Augustinian monastery complex which is not open to the general public.

The interior is surprisingly light, due to the whitewashed walls and large windows, and also quite sparse - though the baroque main altar, dating from 1634, is exquisite (as are the choir stalls); one truly magnificent painting depicts *The Mystical Marriage of St Catherine* (1674).

The other church is the **Pauline Church on the Rock** (*Kościół Paulinów na Skałce*), the rock in question being Skałka, a limestone hill which was the scene of one of the most important episodes in Poland's history: the martyrdom of St Stanisław, the country's patron saint. Originally a Romanesque rotunda stood on this spot, in the thirteenth century this was replaced by a gothic church, which was completely rebuilt in the years 1740-2.

The imposing baroque facade of the church doesn't really prepare you for the intimate interior. The main altar, with an eighteenth century painting of St Michael, undoubtedly plays second fiddle to the altar to the left, traditionally believed to be the spot where Stanisław said his last mass, and where he was killed. The present version of the altar dates from 1745; within the glass case is a piece of the tree trunk upon which it is said the saint's body was decapitated, while through the three small holes in the wall to the right you can just about make out a stone dyed by his blood.

Underneath the church, the **Crypt of Honour** (*Krypta Zasłużonych*) was built in 1880 on the 400th anniversary of the death of the famous Polish historian Jan Długosz (1415-80), whose coffin was moved here. A number of other Polish notables are buried in the crypt including astronomer Tadeusz Banachiewicz (1882-1954), actor Ludwik Solski (1855-1954), poets Wincenty Pol (1807-72), Teofil Lenartowicz (1822-93), Adam Asnyk (1838-97), Lucjan Siemieński (1807-77) and Czesław Miłosz (1911-2004), and painters Jacek

The Martyrdom of St Stanisław

The exact reasons for the dispute between King Bolesław II ("the Bold") and Stanisław Szcezepański, Bishop of Kraków, are not known because there are no contemporary chronicles, but we do know that it ended brutally in 1079 with the bishop's gruesome murder - he had his head chopped off with a mighty sword (some say by the king's own hand), and was then cut up into little pieces.

Stanisław's butchered remains were initially buried in a church on Skałka, before being transferred to Wawel Cathedral in 1088. In 1253 Stanisław was canonised and soon after he was declared Poland's patron saint; Polish kings were crowned in front of his tomb in the cathedral following a traditional pilgrimage to Skałka (the day before the coronation) to atone for his murder. Every year on the Sunday after May 8th, the supposed date of his martyrdom, there is a procession from Wawel to Skałka featuring the toppermost clergy.

Czesław Miłosz

Born in Szetejnie in 1911 in what is today Lithuania, Czesław Miłosz published his first volume of poetry in 1933. In 1945 Miłosz entered the Polish diplomatic service, however, his increasing sense of dissatisfaction with Polish domestic politics following the imposition of the one-party state in December 1948 led him to leave his post at the Paris embassy in January 1951. Staying on in Paris he published his most famous work *The Captive Mind* (1951), a psychological study of those writers who had reached an accommodation with the totalitarian regime (back in Poland Miłosz was branded a non-person and all his books were banned). In 1961 he took up a post at the University of Berkeley in California where he produced a prodigious output of poetry, essays, translations and even a History of Polish literature (1969). In 1980 he was awarded the Nobel Prize for Literature and the following year he was allowed to return to Poland where his less contentious poetic works appeared in print officially for the first time. Miłosz died in 2004 and is buried in the Crypt of Honour underneath the Pauline Church on the Rock.

Malczewski (1854-1929) and Stanisław Wyspiański (1869-1907) - cards in English give details of their lives. The entrance is via the main facade of the church, under the steps.

Next to the church is a pond known as the **Font of Poland**, thought to have been the scene of ritual sacrifices in times gone by. According to legend, St Stanisław's body was dumped here after his murder and so, appropriately, in the centre of the pond is a statue of him (his various body parts are traditionally believed to have miraculously re-united themselves in the pond). The smelly water here is traditionally thought to have curing properties for eye and skin complaints, and there is a tap for anyone feeling brave or ill enough. The wooden cross nearby was put here by Kraków students after a meeting with Pope John Paul II in 1979, on the four hundredth anniversary of the martyrdom of St Stanisław.

South of the Wisła: Podgórze and the Plaszów Labour Camp

In March 1941 the Jewish population of Kraków was moved to a tiny ghetto in the **Podgórze** district, south of the Wisła, centred around **Plac Bohaterów Getta** (Square of the Ghetto Heroes). A 2m (6ft) high wall - it's semi-circular top echoing that of a tombstone - was built to keep them in and all windows facing out of the ghetto were bricked up. Anyone caught entering or leaving the ghetto without permission was immediately killed. Jews were deported from the ghetto to the camps at Treblinka and Auschwitz-Birkenau at regular intervals until the ghetto itself was finally destroyed in March 1943.

At the south-west corner of Plac Bohaterów Getta stands the **Old Ghetto Pharmacy** (*Muzeum Pamięci*

Narodowej), which was open 24 hours a day, seven days a week during the ghetto years and run by the ghetto's only non-Jewish inhabitant, Tadeusz Pankiewicz (who wrote a very interesting account of the war years, which has recently been re-printed, called *The Kraków Ghetto Pharmacy*). The pharmacy was permitted by the Germans because they feared the outbreak of typhoid fever and it very much became a hub of the community. Today it houses an exhibition devoted to the ghetto years; Steven Speilberg and Roman Polański are among those who have donated funds to the museum. On Lwowska, which runs off Plac Bohaterów Getta, is a short section of surviving **ghetto wall**, with a small plaque identifying it as such - there is another surviving section behind the school situated where Wielicka meets Rękawka.

Oscar Schindler's Factory is still standing nearby at Lipowa 4. Built in 1937 as a metal works factory, it produced enamelware when Schindler ran it from 1940-4 and the exterior looks pretty much the same as it did in Schindler's day (give or take a few sign changes). A printing works presently

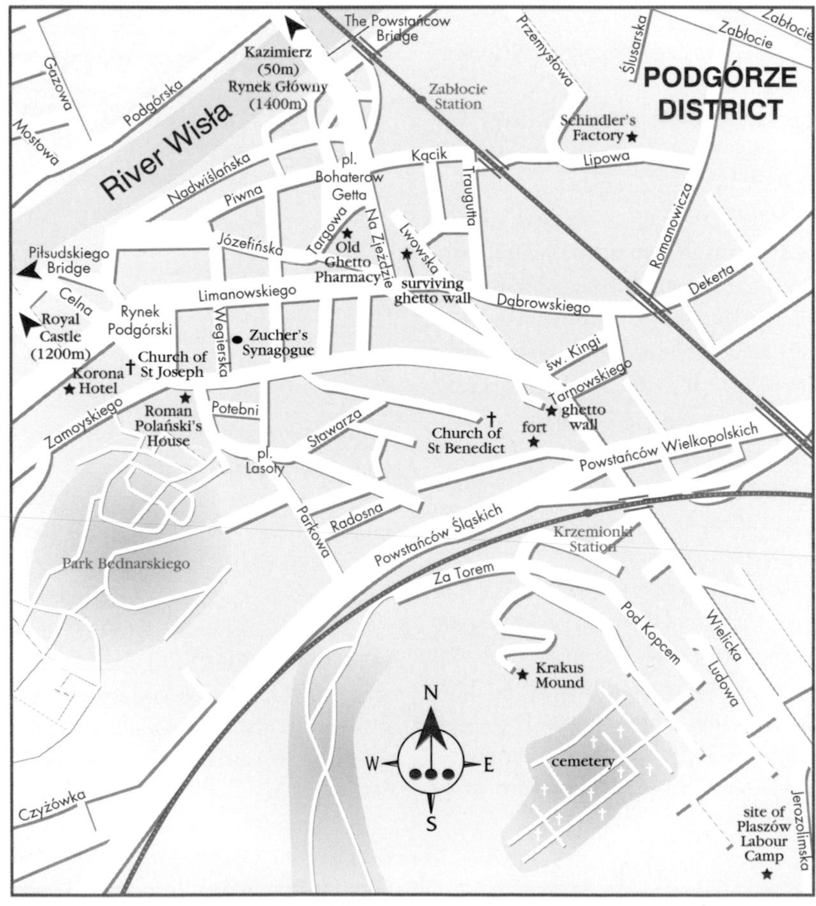

The Rumuh Cemetery, originally dates from the 1550s

Roman Polański

Film director Roman Polański was born in Paris in 1933 to a Polish father and Russian mother. Although his father was Jewish and his mother half-Jewish, they were not religiously observant, but because of rising anti-semitism in France the family decided to move to Kraków in 1937. After the Nazi invasion they were resettled, with several other families, at Rękawka 2 in the Podgórze district and in his autobiography *Roman by Polański* Polański recounts watching the construction of the Podgórze Ghetto wall from his window. With his father's help, Polański managed to escape the ghetto on the day it was liquidated and he subsequently survived with the help of a local Catholic family (both of his parents were sent to concentration camps, his mother dying in Auschwitz, something Polański only found out after the war had ended).

In his teens Polański acted in a number of Polish films (including Wajda's *Generation*). After turning his hand to direction, he gained an immediate international reputation with his first full-length feature *Knife in the Water* (1962), which was nominated for an Oscar for best foreign language film. Polański then left Poland for England where he made the arthouse horror classic *Repulsion* (1965), starring Catherine Deneuve. Subsequent successes include *Rosemary's Baby* (1968), *Chinatown* (1974) and *The Pianist* (2002) which recounted Polish Jew Władysław Szpilman's battle for survival in Warsaw during the Second World War (Steven Speilberg had originally asked Polański to film *Schindler's List* but he turned down the offer). *The Pianist* went on to win the Palm d'Or at the Cannes Fim Festival and Polański also picked up the Best Director award at the Oscars.

Oscar Schindler

Schindler (1908 -1974 was an enigmatic, ambivalent figure who is credited - rightly - with saving hundreds of Kraków Jews from certain death in the concentration camps, but whose motives for doing so have been the subject of considerable controversy. Of Austrian descent he was born into a Catholic German-speaking family in Zvitavy (Zwittau), in what was then Czechoslavakia.

He became a Nazi in the 1930s; and in 1938 he was arrested by the Czech authorities for the spying for the Nazis, but was released after the German invasion of the then Czechoslavakia. It is believed that Schindler took part in the fake 'incursions' into German territory in September 1939, which the Germans staged with German soldiers dressed up as Poles in order to claim an excuse for the invasion of Poland.

Wartime

A few months after the outbreak of World War II, Schindler was running a kitchenware factory in Cracow as a cover for some heavy black-market trading. His easy charm and magnetic personality led to him forming many contacts with top Nazi officials in the city, and these contacts got him out of jail on a number of occasions when he faced accusations of black marketeering (for which he could, in theory, have been executed).

He was notorious as a lover of fast cars, women, drink and money. In particular he was a friend of the highest-ranking and most feared Nazi figure in Cracow, Amon Goeth, who ran the forced labour camp of Plaszów on the outskirts of the city (and was later executed for war crimes in Cracow in 1946). The camp was built on the site of a former Jewish cemetery, which the Nazis obliterated in a wanton act of destruction, forcing Cracow Jews to desecrate the graves of their forefathers by making them use tombstones to construct roads in the camp.

Goeth lived in a purpose-built villa overlooking the site; from his terrace he would shoot prisoners at random. Schindler meanwhile grew rich through his business activities and the use of Jewish slave labour in his Cracow factory, the Deutsche Emailwaren Fabrik, known to its workers as 'Emalia', which soon began to make munitions for the German war effort.

Destruction of the ghetto

On March 13th 1943 the Cracow ghetto was liquidated; 2000 died there as the Nazis cleared the place, and the remaining inhabitants were sent to Auschwitz or to work in appalling conditions at Plaszów. Schindler was warned of the impending liquidation of the ghetto by his Nazi contacts, and made his workers sleep in his factory for three nights so that they were spared. He then set up his own 'concentration camp' in the factory grounds, which was free of SS involvement and where Jews were not subject to arbitrary punishments or cruel and degrading treatment. He kept officialdom at bay by bribing leading Nazis with black market diamonds, and through protection by the German Armaments Protectorate for whom his workers were manufacturing weapons.

Move to Czechoslovakia

In September 1944 the Nazis forced the closure of his factory as Poland became threatened by advancing Soviet forces. Schindler insisted that his factory was vital to the war effort and told the Nazis that he wanted to keep his Jewish workers. He was told in return that he could move production to Brnenec (Brinnlitz) in Czechoslovakia, close to his childhood home in Zvitavy, a hilly, remote region on the borders of Bohemia and Moravia, which was regarded by the Nazis as a safer location for arms production.

He begged to take 1100 specialist Jewish workers with him from Paszów and from his Cracow factory: this was his famous 'list', and those that were on it were saved from certain death in Auschwitz-Birkenau. Some of the women on his list were transported, by accident or design of Nazi authorities, to Birkenau, where they remained for three weeks until Schindler persuaded the Nazis that they were his workers and should be set free. They were the only group of prisoners ever to be released from Birkenau during its three-year history.

In Brinnlitz, Schindler made sure his workers were looked after properly and treated humanely. The SS were kept at bay by Oscar's bribes and contacts, by the remoteness of the site, and by the pressure on the German armed forces as the war dragged to a close. Schindler risked his life constantly for the sake of his prisoners, even going so far as to establish a Jewish cemetery near the camp for those who died during the fearsome winter of 1944-5. He also made sure that the armaments his factory made were inferior and useless to the German war effort.

On the last day of the war Schindler rigged up speakers in his Brinnlitz factory so that his workers could hear Churchill's victory speech, broadcast live from London. A number of his workers helped him escape to American-occupied Czechoslovakia, fearing that the Russians, who had liberated Brinnlitz, would execute Schindler as a Nazi (which of course is what he was – in theory).

After the war

After 1945 he was involved in a number of failed business ventures in Germany and Argentina, and he eventually finished up living in a tiny apartment opposite Frankfurt railway station. He became a frequent visitor to Israel where he was the recipient of many gifts from Holocaust survivor groups, and was made a 'Righteous Person' by the Israeli government. He died in poverty – and largely of drink – in 1974 in his Frankfurt apartment. His funeral service was held in the Catholic Church of Mount Zion, Jerusalem, where he was buried.

Schindler's motives remain unclear to this day. Some have suggested that he was more interested in making money out of his factory and profiting from the availability of Jewish slave labour, than actually saving Jews from the Birkenau gas chambers. Yet, even if he emerged a hero by accident rather than design, it is impossible not to recognize his achievements during the blackest days of the Holocaust.

His intriguing and fascinating story was told by Thomas Keneally in his 1982 Booker Prize-winning novel *Schindler's Ark*; in it he describes his hero as 'a sentimentalist who loved the transparency, the simplicity of doing good ... [he was] by temperament an anarchist who loved to ridicule the system.' The book was memorably filmed by Steven Spielberg in 1994 as *Schindler's List*, one of the most impressive (and certainly the most widely-seen) films ever made about the Holocaust. Spielberg used actual Cracow locations, including the ghetto streets and Schindler's old factory, in the making of the film, which was the recipient of many awards, including the Oscar for best film.

The Old Synagogue, a focal point of the city's Jewish Quarter, dating from the 1570s

The Filming of *Schindler's List*

Steven Spielberg first came to Kraków, scouting out locations for *Schindler's List*, in 1992, and he immediately became determined to use the city as an authentic stage for the very real events depicted in the film. Szeroka, at the heart of Jewish Kazimierz, doubled for Plac Bohaterów Getta in the Podgórze Ghetto (the latter's character having changed considerably since the war). The surrounding streets were also heavily used; in particular the courtyard between Józefa and Meiselsa (located next to the Jewish Cultural Centre) during the scenes depicting the liquidation of the ghetto. The bridge the Jews crossed when being relocated to the Podgórze Ghetto is the one at the end of Krakówska (although Speilberg filmed them walking the "wrong" way).

The most obvious setting used south of the Wisła was Schindler's actual factory at Lipowa 4. The entrance gate is seen in the film on numerous occasions, though the interior shots were taken elsewhere. The scene where Schindler is riding his horse and witnessing the liquidation of the ghetto was filmed nearby on the Lasoty Hill, which features a wonderful Austrian fort (regrettably not open to the public) dating to 1852, and a small sixteenth century church dedicated to St Benedict. The Płaszów Camp was rebuilt in a quarry at the bottom of the Krakus Mound off the road Za Torem. Thirty-four barracks and eleven watchtowers were constructed as well as a narrow gauge railway and the famous tombstone road. Designer Allan Starski (who worked for many years with Andrzej Wajda) won one of the film's seven Oscars, for set design and art direction, for his work here.

occupies part of the interior but there is also an exhibition commemorating the events of the last war, and there are plans to turn the whole complex into a huge modern art gallery. A short walk away from Plac Bohaterów Getta, at Węgierska 5 is the **Zucher's Synagogue**, built 1879-81 which now houses a very swish private art gallery. The large church that stands at the southern end of the main square in Podgórze, Rynek Podgórski, is dedicated to St Joseph; it has a very striking Disney-like neo-Gothic appearance but is not actually very old - dating only to 1909.

The **Plaszów Labour Camp** was located a little to the south of the Podgórze district, in the area between the two main arteries Wielicka and Kamieńskiego; look for the two martyrs' memorial symbols marked on official city maps. The camp was built on the site of two Jewish cemeteries (and its roads made from their tombstones); it was completely destroyed by the Nazis in the weeks before the arrival of the Soviet army here on January 15th 1945. The best way to approach it is along Jerozololimska. The grey house that you see standing alone functioned as the SS headquarters and its cellars were used as torture chambers. Further along, Jerozolimska becomes Heltmana and the house at 22 belonged to Amon Goeth, the commander of the camp, who used to shoot at prisoners from his balcony here. Back at the grey house, there once used to be a road that ran from here through the middle of the camp called Abrahama - it is still marked on city maps, though today it is just a trail. Follow this trail westwards through the main camp area; up on the hill to your right are a few remaining Jewish tombstones (one of which just about stands upright), while if you carry on straight ahead you will see looming on the horizon to your left a large square monument which commemorates all the unknown Jews who died here.

On a lighter note, on the way to the site of the camp, just off Wielicka, is the **Krakus Mound** (*Kopiec Kraka*), a popular picnic spot which offers a great view back to the city (if you can manage to climb the steep sides to the top!). The mound is about 10 metres high and excavations have revealed that it once had an oak tree on top; thought to date from the seventh century, legend has it that this is the burial place of King Krak.

near the Old Synagogue

A history of Jews in Kraków

The first wave of Jewish settlers came to Kraców in 1304, a result of the population migrations caused by the Black Death. They settled in a quarter of the city around present day sw. Anny, and a synagogue, bath house, wedding house and hospital were built. In 1335 Kazimierz the Great established the town of Kazimierz (named after him) next to Kraców, and it was here that the Jewish community went when they were expelled from Kraców in 1495, the scapegoats for a major fire that devastated the town.

In 1533 a separate Jewish town was established within Kazimierz, which was surrounded by a wall with three gates. Kazimierz became very prosperous, benefiting greatly from the trade that passed through Kraców, and by the sixteenth century it had the largest concentration of Jews in Europe. However the town suffered terrible destruction during the Swedish invasion of the 1650s and around two-thirds of Kazimierz's Jews emigrated - mainly to Warsaw.

By the time Kazimierz became incorporated into Kraców, in 1800, Jews still made up around a third of its population – and it seems that Jews and non-Jews lived harmoniously together, with many Jews living in the traditional Christian half of Kazimierz. During the nineteenth century the more wealthy Jews moved to the heart of Kraców (Floriańska was even nicknamed 'Jewish Street'), and the traditional Jewish quarter of Kazimierz became one of the poorest areas of the city.

During World War II virtually the entire Jewish community of around 64,000 (a quarter of the city's population) was murdered. German troops entered Kraców on 14 September 1939. On 18 November all Jews were forced to identify themselves by wearing armbands bearing the Star of David. In March 1941 an official ghetto was built to the south of the river in the Podgórze district; all Kraców's Jews were forcibly rehoused into some 320 buildings there.

June 1942 saw the first deportations to the nearby concentration camps, and in November a labour camp was established at Plaszów, a little to the south of the city. On March 14th 1943 the Podgórze Ghetto was liquidated, its remaining population either being killed or transported to Auschwitz.

At the end of the war around 6000 Jews returned to settle in Kraców, but over the years the community dwindled as its younger members decamped either to Israel or the USA. It is only since the end of Communism that the city's Jewish past is being acknowledged and commemorated – largely due, it must be said, to the success of Steven Spielberg's film, Schindler's List, which was filmed here.

Places to visit in Stradom, Kazimierz and Podgórze

Ethnographic Museum
Plac Wolnica
Open: Mon 10am-6pm; Wed-Fri 10am-3pm; Sat and Sun 10am-2pm

Museum of Municipal Engineering
Św Wawrzyńca 15
Open: Tue-Sun 10am-4pm

High Synagogue
Józefa 38
Open: Mon-Sun 9am-5pm

Old Synagogue
Szeroka 24
Open: Mon 10am-2pm;Tue-Sun 10am-5pm (9am-4pm in winter)

Rumuh Synagogue and Cemetery
Szeroka 46
Open: Sun-Fri 9am-4pm

Galicia Jewish Museum
Dajwór 18
Open: Mon-Sun 9.30am-5.30pm

Popper Synagogue
Szeroka 16
Open: Mon-Fri 9am-2pm and 4-6pm

New Jewish Cemetery
Miodowa 55
Open: Mon-Thu 10am-5pm (3pm in winter); Fri 10am-2pm

Isaac Synagogue
Kupa 18
Open: Sun-Fri 9am-7pm

Jewish Cultural Centre
Meiselsa 17
Open: Sun-Fri 10am-6pm

Tempel Synagogue
Miodowa 24
Open: Sun-Fri 10am-6pm

Old Ghetto Pharmacy
Plac Bohaterów Getta 13
Open: Mon 10am-2pm; Tue-Sat 9.30am-5pm (9am-4pm in winter)

4. Excursions from the City

The places described in this chapter are all within relatively easy travelling distance of the centre of Kraków. The chapter is structured so that those places that are closest to the city centre are described first, followed by other destinations that make good day or half-day trips but which take an hour or two to reach by train or road from the city.

The following places can be reached by the city's bus and tram network, using the same tickets which cover the services within the city centre (see p.151); all are shown on the recommended city map, *Kraków: Plan Miasta* (see p.141).

Opposite: Visitors at the former concentration camp of Auschwitz

Below: Carving in salt of King Kazimierz, Wieliczka Salt Mine

Firstly the **Wieliczka salt mine** must be the most popular excursion from Kraków, with its subterranean journey through a seven-hundred-year old mine where natural forces have carved huge caverns and strange shapes from the natural salt formations. Kraków's industrial suburb of **Nowa Huta** makes for a less obvious tourist attraction, but is nonetheless fascinating; here mile upon mile of grey apartment blocks – forming an enticingly different urban landscape to the medieval icing-cake of the city centre – surround Poland's largest steel works, an iconic feature from communist days that still dominates the economy and urban landscape of eastern Kraków. In the city's eastern suburbs you'll find the outdoor **aviation museum**, whilst over in Kraków's western fringes the **zoo** and a historic viewpoint known as the **Kościuszko Mound** are located amidst the appealing surroundings of villa-strewn woodland. The **Wolski Forest**, which offers opportunities for very pleasant walks (see p.102), extends from the zoo and the Kościuszko Mound as far as the strange, forbidding monastery of **Bielany**, situated to the west of the city overlooking the River Wisła; a second monastery, **Tyniec**, lies on a rocky bluff above the opposite bank.

Visitors to Kraków with more time on their hands might want to venture further afield. Reasonably close at hand is **Wadowice**, around 50 kilometres to the southwest of Kraków, which is the home town of Pope John Paul II. Three other possible destinations require more time and effort to reach, and all lie around 100 kilometres from the city. **Częstochowa,** to the northwest, is Poland's greatest site of Catholic pilgrimage; **Zakopane**, to the south, is the country's most popular mountain resort, with skiing, hiking and cable-car rides on offer; while just to the east of Zakopane, the **Dunajec Gorge** is the setting for some spectacular rafting trips along a mountain river. Finally, the former Nazi concentration camp of **Auschwitz**, 80km west of the city, is the most worthwhile long-distance excursion, and is covered in the chapter that follows this one.

For those who do not wish to travel independently, a variety of travel agencies in Kraków (see p.150) organize guided tours from the city by coach to all these destinations and many others (including Warsaw).

The Wieliczka Salt Mine

Don't be put off by the sheer idea of going on a visit to a salt mine; this is an absorbing and highly recommended day trip from the city. The **Wieliczka Salt Mine** (*kopalnia soli*) is not some unappetising hangover from the communist era, it has been in operation for over 700 years and the place is even included on UNESCO's World Cultural Heritage List.

The statistics alone are awesome; some 300km (186 miles) of underground tunnels stretch over an area of 10 square kilometres (6 square miles), while nine levels of mining reach down to a depth of over 320m. Yet statistics alone cannot convey the experience of visiting the mine.

Entry is by official **tour** only, you pay for the guide and your ticket at the ticket office; the placc is very popular so there will be crowds in summer when you should arrive early if you can. Tours start every 10 minutes or so in summer and about every 40 minutes in winter; English tours are available roughly every 30 minutes in July and August, and about every hour outside of those months. The tour itself takes around two hours and there is a fifteen minute break in the middle. A word of advice: it's worth taking a jumper in summer as the temperature in the mine is an all year round 14C (conversely, of course, the mine is a relatively warm place to be in winter).

Initially you descend a steep stairway deep into the ground; although only 1% of the mine is explored (a trip around the whole lot would take

Zbigniew Preisner

Zbigniew Preisner (b.1955) is one of the world's most outstanding film composers. Probably best known for his collaborations with the director Krzysztof Kieślowski, he achieved his big international break with his score for the film *The Double Life of Veronique*, which was partially filmed in Kraków (in the film frequent reference is made to the composer Van Den Budenmayer, though this is just Preisner in disguise). The soundtrack of the film has sold over 300,000 copies, while the soundtrack albums for the *Three Colours Trilogy* have sold a total of 700,000 copies. Preisner originally read history and philosophy at the University of Kraków and studied music only in his spare time, yet despite being self-taught he has gone on to achieve outstanding success; in the 1990s alone he composed scores for seventeen different films as varied as *When a Man Loves a Woman*, *The Secret Garden* and *Damage*. In 1998 he produced *Requiem for my Friend*, his first large scale non-film work, a farewell to Kieślowski who died in 1996. Preisner continues to live part-time in Kraków where he has his own studio and even his own website (www.preisner.com).

four months) it's a long and eventually quite tiring tour, but generally it gets better the further you go on. Apart from the strange natural formations (including odd string-like salt drippings from the ceilings), there are spectacular underground lakes, numerous carvings (undertaken by the miners themselves) and the jewel in the crown, the huge **Blessed Kinga's Chapel** (*Kaplica Błogosławionej Kingi*), which was carved completely out of salt in the early nineteenth century; note especially the fantastic **relief of the Last Supper**, a triumph of perspective for something only eight inches deep. Banquets, weddings and sometimes even concerts are held in the chapel; one of the most memorable was by Zbigniew Preisner who arranged his film music into a special suite for the occasion, which was recorded and is available on a CD called *Preisner's Music*. A **museum** at the lower level is dedicated to the history of the mine (ask your guide at the end of the official tour, as you'll have to buy a separate ticket at the bottom). You'll be relieved to know that there is a lift to take you back up to the surface and that, conveniently, minibuses back to Kraków congregate outside the exit.

Local trains from Kraków's main railway station wend their way only infrequently to the town of Wieliczka, so the easisest way to get there is by taking one of the frequent minibuses that run from the scruffy bus station on Worcella, 200m west of the railway station - you can also pick them up along Starowiślna, or from the end of Grodzka (near the *Hotel Royal*). The journey time is around 30 minutes and the bus has Wieliczka's name prominently displayed on it. The bus stops right outside the mine which is signposted in English anyway all over the town. The mine is open daily from 7.30am - 7.30pm (8am - 5pm, November to March) and there is a 20% discount in winter.

Nowa Huta

10km east of the old city lies the suburb of **Nowa Huta** (which translates literally as "New Steelworks"), a part of Kraków's past (and present) that most Cracovians would prefer not to be re-

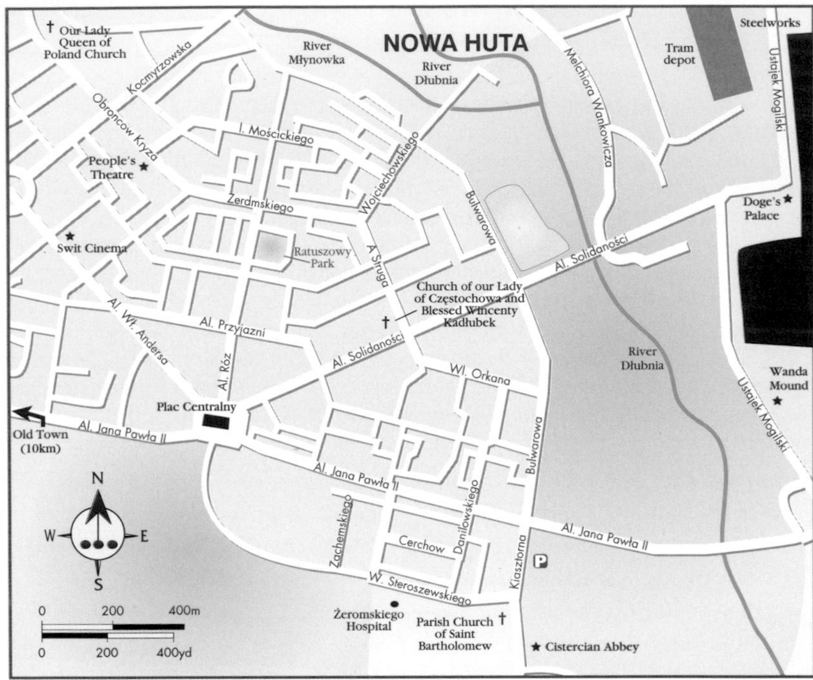

minded about. When the Communists came to power in post-war Poland they deemed Kraków's cultural and religious roots as potentially problematic so they set about industrializing the city and dramatically changing its social make-up. A gigantic steelworks was built (originally called the Lenin Steelworks but now renamed after the metallurgist Tadeusz Sendzimir) along with a completely new "ideal" town of wide boulevards and tower blocks to house the new proletariat (and all this despite the fact that there are no natural resources here - the ore had to be imported from the Ukraine). In 1951 15,000 people lived in Nowa Huta - nowadays the number is nearer 250,000.

Since the end of Communism many parts of the steelworks have been closed down for either financial or environmental reasons (pollution has contributed severely to health problems of Kraków's inhabitants and the decay of many of the city's monuments), causing widespread unemployment within the Nowa Huta district. Nowa Huta is perhaps not the most aesthetically pleasing of Kraków's many districts but a visit to the suburb is in many ways essential to understanding Kraków's - and indeed Poland's - recent past.

Trams 4 and 15, which leave from Basztowa, just south-west of the main railway station, take you to **plac Centralny**, Nowa Huta's main square, which is surrounded by some very grand Renaissance and Baroque-influenced buildings; the square was designed to compete with the great urban centres of Europe and is now a world heritage site. The southern side is open; a huge theatre was originally going to be constructed here, but it was never built - and the spire that was going to stand in the middle of the square was never erected either. A huge statue of Lenin did however once stand on the avenue leading north from the square, aleja Róz; some locals attempted to blow it up in 1979, but only succeeded in dislodging part of the statue's foot (along with most of the neighbouring windows) - after the fall of Communism the statue was sold to a Swedish businessman and it now resides in a park near Vąrnamo.

For anybody interested in the so-called **Social Realist** style of architecture (see box), there are a couple of good examples within walking distance of the main square; the **Swit Cinema** on Andersa resembles a huge Classical temple, while the similarly grand **People's Theatre** (*Teatr Ludowy*) on Obrońoców Krzyza (which was built in 1954 in place of the one earmarked for the southern side of plac Centralny) has an exceedingly good reputation for the performances contained within. A bit further out, the administrative centre of the steelworks, situated at the entrance at Ujastek 1, borrows many elements from the Italian Renaissance style and is commonly called the **Doge's Palace** - the gables directly echo those on the Sukiennice on Rynek Główny.

It's worth checking out the interesting (and wildly contrasting) **churches** in the area. No churches were included in the original plans for Nowa Huta and their construction was forbidden by the Communist authorities until increasingly violent protests eventually led to a relaxation of the ban. By far the most impressive of the churches is the **Our Lady Queen of Poland Church** (*Kościół N.M.P. Królowej Polski Arka*) on Obrońoców Krzyza, which was built largely by hand by the local populas over ten years and was finally consecrated in 1977. The church is in the shape of a huge ark and it's either a concrete and glass masterpiece or monstrocity depending on your point of view; the interior is hardly very intimate but there is a huge and bizarrely fascinating sculpture of Jesus on the cross (though it looks like he's figure-skating) in the main hall. Also worth a look is the **Church of Our Lady of Częstochowa and Blessed Wincenty Kadłubek** (*Kościół Matki Boskiej Częstochowskiej*) on Struga which was erected in the 1980s; the huge glass roof looks as if it was designed by Picasso during his cubist period.

Nowa Huta possesses two churches which are very much older than these however, being in the former village of Mogiła, which is only about a twenty minute walk east from plac Centralny. They stand opposite each other along Klasztorna. The magnificent **Cistercian Abbey** (*Opactwo Cystersów*) here was founded back in 1222, while the adjoining **Church of the Virgin Mary and St Wenceslas** was consecrated in 1266 - it was rebuilt in the baroque style in the eighteenth century. The door of the church is usually left open and it conceals a very colourful interior with an array of bright yellows, blues and greens unusual in a place of worship; the gothic pointed arches are an obvious remnant from the church's initial construction. Note the polyptych (dating from 1514) which adorns the altar and also the murals in the chancel and transept which date from the sixteenth century and were painted by one of the abbey's monks. A door leads from the church into the cloisters, which date to the fourteenth century. Opposite the abbey is the small wooden **parish church of St Bartholomew** (*Kościół Św Bartłomieja*), constructed completely of wood by the royal carpenter Maciej Mączka in 1466; unusually for a wooden church it has three aisles, but unfortunately the building is kept locked outside of the Sunday service.

Not too far away from these, in the direction of the steelworks off Mogilski, Nowa Huta boasts its own mound, the **Wanda Mound** (*Kopiec Wandy*), thought to date to around the seventh century and, according to legend, the finally resting place ofWanda, daughter of Krak, who is said to have become ruler of Kraków after her two brothers died in a dispute over the succession. The story goes that Wanda offered to sacrifice herself if her people were successful in fending off the raid of a German prince, and when they did just that rather than conveniently forgetting her oath she drowned herself in the Wisła - the mound is said to mark the spot where her body was washed up. In 1890 a monument to her, topped by a white eagle, was placed on top.

Anybody who finds Nowa Huta fascinating rather than off-putting (it's possible) and who wants to explore the place in greater detail should seek out the local pocket guide *Kraków's Nowa Huta* published by Bezdroża, which is a highly informative and entertaining read.

Monasteries on the River Wisła West of Kraków

West of Kraków the Wisła heads through some attractive countryside, sprinkled with farms, villas and villages. Two baroque monasteries overlook the river just outside the city and visiting them makes for a pleasant morning or afternoon trip out from the city. **Bielany**, on the north bank 6km (4 miles) west of the castle, can be reached by bus and a walk of 10—15 minutes; **Tyniec**, which overlooks the south bank of the river 8km (5 miles) west of the city, can be reached by bus. Both are working monasteries and you may not be able to visit at certain times; the positions of both are marked on the *Kraków: Plan Miasta* map (see p.141).

Tyniec Monastery

The Benedictine order founded **Tyniec Monastery** *(klasztor Benedyktynow)* on a steep, easily defended bluff of rock overlooking the Wisła river, 10km southwest of the city centre, in 1044. The monks probably came here on the invitation of King Kazimierz the Restorer, and the site he offered them was probably that of a former fortress. That first church was destroyed in 1240 during the Tartar invasion; another church was built in the fifteenth century (when the defensive walls, modelled on the Wawel defences, were added) and much of the interior was remodelled in Baroque style between 1618 and 1622. A chequered history led the monastery to fall into disuse in the nineteenth century, but in the last

A retreat in the hills

The ascetic, meditative order of the Camadolese monks at Bielany has been a source of fascination for centuries. The Order was founded in Italy by St Romuald around a thousand years ago; today there are only eight Camadolese hermitages in the world, in Poland, Italy and Colombia. The founder of Bielany, Marshal Mikołaj Wolski, was a highly educated man who dabbled in alchemy and other unorthodox ways of making money before realizing the error of his ways and repenting his sins in front of Pope Clement III. The Pope told Wolski he should found a new monastery with all the money he had. Wolski chose the remote hillside above the Wisła River as a suitable home for a religious order dedicated to silence and seclusion. The church and hermitage were completed in 1642.

Wolski nonetheless considered himself a great sinner, hence his decision to be buried (wearing his monks attire) in a spot which will make people walk over him all the time. Today, the order he founded still lives and worships according to the rules of hard work (mostly in the monastery vegetable garden), poverty and lack of private property laid down by Wolski. Monks live as hermits, in virtual seclusion, eating meals alone apart from at certain religious festivals. There is an induction and initiation process lasting over five years for those who consider that such a life is for them.

Although the legend that monks sleep in coffins with bricks as pillows is not true, there is no doubt that Bielany is a gloomy, melancholic place, no more so than down in the crypt where bodies of former monks are bricked up behind niches which record the date they died, their name and age. When the bodies are finally removed from the crypt the bones are moved to an anonymous place in the monastery ossuary, and the name disappears from the niche: a final act of humility.

hundred years the building has been restored. The community of monks has moved back and now there are six services daily in the church.

The whole place is hushed and very sober, and the church has none of the ornate or luxurious decorations of Kraków churches: the high altar, fashioned from black marble in the mid eighteenth century by Francesco Placidi, the choir stalls painted with scenes from the life of St Benedict, and the rococo pulpit shaped like the prow of a boat, are its most striking elements. The church is the setting for a series of famed organ recitals given on selected days during the early summer (see page 137), which are in fact the principal reason for coming here, as the buildings themselves are rather bleak and some of the monastic part

Social Realism

Social Realism was an artistic movement whose concern was the working classes, standpoint was left-wing and aim was to celebrate the proletariat and to encourage them in the struggle to form a perfect socialist state. It essentially emerged in the Soviet Union the 1930s and died with its fall in 1991. Painters and sculptors were "encouraged" to take up as their theme the struggle of the working classes, and to present their activities in an heroic manner. In terms of architecture, it was important for buildings to be on a monumental scale in order to express the power of the state, and also its mass collective nature; in Poland, Social Realism came to include many elements of the Renaissance style, which was deemed to be the most characteristic element of Polish architecture.

Tyniec Monastery, a medieval foundation on the River Wisła

Walks in the Wolski Forest

The Wolski Forest, lying to the west of the city, is an ideal setting for numerous walks amidst forested and sometimes craggy hills. Walking tracks are colour-coded and marked on the *Kraków: Plan Miasta* map as a series of dashed lines; out in the forest, the walks are signposted and marked *en route* by coloured markers painted on trees and walls. Starting points and destinations include the Kościuszko Mound (p.105); the zoo (p.103); another mound, Piłsudskiego, created in the 1930s to honour the Poles who died in the various campaigns for Polish independence that took place throughout the nineteenth century, and named after the politican and general Josef Piłsudski (see p.000); a reconstructed sixteenth century timber church, located just north of the zoo (on Cisowa street and marked on maps as a "skansen", ie an open air museum); and the Bielany Monastery.

of the complex is partly ruined and inaccessible (although the view across the broad valley of the Wisła from the courtyard is a fine one).

Tyniec is close enough to Kraków to be shown in detail on the recommended city map, *Kraków: Plan Miasta* (see p.141). Coming here by city bus number 112 is straight-forward: pick it up from the stops adjacent to the busy roundabout at the western end of the Grunwaldzki bridge in the centre of Kraków (trams 18, 19 and 22 stop here). In Tyniec itself, a prosperous commuter village, get off the bus as it turns abruptly left, and take the lane which leads off to the right; it's a five minute stroll along Benedyktynska, a quiet residential road. During weekends in Summer, boat trips used to operate from below Wawel Castle to a landing stage adjacent to the monastery, but these were discontinued in 1999: however it might be worth asking at the tourist office in Kraków whether they have resumed in recent years.

The Aviation Museum and the zoo

Two unusual destinations in the Kraków suburbs are the aviation museum and the zoo; the locations of both are marked on the *Kraków: Plan Miasta* map and both can be reached on the city public transport network. The former, the *Muzeum Lotnictwa Polskiego*, is located in the eastern suburb of Czyzyny on the site of Poland's first ever airfield, and is largely open-air. On display are dozens of fighter and civilian aircraft and helicopters from 1915 onwards, including a Russian 1917 flying boat and some elderly LOT passenger planes manufactured by the old Soviet rival to Boeing, Tupolev. Inside is a huge collection of aircraft engines, the oldest of which dates from 1908. The museum is open from May 1st to November 30th from 9am to 3pm daily except Monday (opening time at the weekend is 10am); those who turn up outside these times may well be able to wander round the open-air section. The museum is unfortunately confusingly signposted. To reach it, follow Mogilska Street, one of the main traffic arteries running east from the city centre, and take the road on the left after Ulanów, immediately past the school. Trams 4,5 and 15 run from Basztowa, near the Barbican, to a stop close to the museum on Mogilska.

The *Ogrod Zoologiczny*, founded in 1929, is located in the Wolski forest to the west of the city and can be reached by bus 134 which runs up from the *Cracovia* hotel and terminates a hundred metres or so from the zoo entrance. Open daily, the zoo is very pleasingly situated amidst trees; the names of the animals are given in English but otherwise the only language in use is Polish. There are plenty of local animals such as bison, wild boar and lynx, and also many birds, big cats (though not lions), wolves and sealions; some of the animals look as if they could do with more room in their cages. The reptile house, with snakes, tropical fish, tortoises and iguanas makes for a warm retreat on a cold day. The zoo is the start of a number of walks through the attractive Wolski Forest.

Bielany Monastery

Travelling out to Tyniec you can see the church and hermitage of **Bielany Monastery** *(Kościół i Erem Kamedułów)* across the river. It is a much darker, more sombre place than Tyniec, brooding amidst trees on a rocky hillock overlooking the valley. The monastery is the preserve of the Camadolese order of monks, who colonised the area in the early seventeenth century. Their church and hermitage is an interesting place to visit, remote and secluded by forest yet less than an hour away from the centre of Kraków; a trek out here gives visitors a good idea of the devoutly Catholic nature of this part of Poland, and also a good glimpse

The Kościuszko Mound, commemorating a Polish national hero, rises above an ancient monastery

of the Polish countryside.

The 20 or so monks go out of their way to keep themselves to themselves, living in separate cells (which you can see around the church) and having little contact with other monks, let alone with the world outside (there's no TV or radio). Communal meals are rare, but you will see monks scuttling around the walled-in complex or singing plainsong in the church, dressed in cream-coloured robes.

The church itself, approached by a narrow walled walkway, is impressively imposing, particularly its massive white limestone facade. Inside the front door, the main tomb you can see is that of the founder of the church, Mikołaj Wolski, placed near the entrance with the deliberate intention that people will walk over it (humbling, perpetually, the tomb's incumbent). You can see his portrait too, hanging on the wall close by. Otherwise, the most noteworthy decoration inside the church is a series of paintings by Tomasso Dolabella depicting the lives of St Benedict and St Romuald, set around the walls of a chapel dedicated to them; the latter saint, who died in Italy during the eleventh century, is the founder of the order.

If the crypt of the church is open you can see niches where the bodies of deceased monks are kept for 80 years before removal to the ossuary; the motto of this strange monastic order is *Memento Mori* – "remember that you must die" – and here in the crypt of their chapel, death is hard to forget.

To reach the monastery, take bus 109, 209, 229 or 239 from Tadeusza Kościuszki, the main road running along the river west and out of the city. You can get off at the Srebrna Góra stop and take the path which leads up the hill from there. It's a 15 – 20 minute walk up through the silent forest, the path swinging left, below and around the monastery walls before leading up to the entrance. It's also possible to walk to the monastery through the forest from the zoo or the Kościuszko Mound. Alternatively there's vehicle access to the monastery from the eastern edge of Bielany village, after the main road has reached the top of the hill (the turning is obvious, but not signposted, and you can leave or pick up the city bus from a stop just beyond it).

Opening hours are from 9am – 11am and 3.00pm to 4.30pm (5pm in summer). In theory only men are allowed inside the church, with women admitted on major festival days, which are 7 February, 25 March, Easter Sunday, Sunday and Monday of Pentecost, Corpus Christi, 19 June, Sunday after 19 June, 15 August, 8 September, 8 December and Christmas Day. Both men and women can attend Mass at 7 or 10am on Sunday.

Wadowice

This small town fifty kilometers south-west of Kraków would still be languishing in quiet obscurity were it not for the election in October 1978 of Karol Wojtyła to the Papacy. Wojtyła was born and grew up in Wadowice and today the place is besieged by an army of the curious and the faithful, who come to pray at the church where Wojtyła prayed and was baptised, to look around his childhood home, and perhaps to buy a Pope John Paul II calendar as a

The Kościuszko Mound

The Kościuszko Mound *(Kopiec T.Kościuszki)* is a 300m (1000ft) high hill located immediately west of the city centre. The mound is a memorial to Tadeusz Kościuszko (1746 – 1817), well-known as a nationalist fighter in both the United States (where he fought against the British in the American War of Independence, playing a prominent part in the Battle of Saratoga and the blockade of Charleston, and later being made an honorary US citizen) and in Poland (where he led the nationalist military insurrection against the Russians, following his public swearing of an Oath of National Uprising in the Rynek Glówny in 1794). Kościuszko touted Republican and populist ideas, influenced by the ideals of independence and liberty of revolutionary France, and he became something of a Polish national hero. Although Polish forces under his command were victorious over the Russians at the Battle of Raclawice in April 1794, they were defeated later on in the same year near Warsaw by a much larger Russian and Prussian army, and Kościuszko was captured and imprisoned in St Petersburg. Later in his life he negotiated with Napoleon and the Russian Tsar over Poland's political future, but failed to repeat the victories that had characterized the earlier part of his life. He died in Switzerland in 1817 and is buried in Wawel Cathedral.

The mound that honours him was built in the 1820s, continuing a tradition of building mounds in and around Kraków which first began in pagan times (recently it has been suggested that Pope John Paul II should be honoured with one of these mounds). No-one is sure what all those original mounds, most of which are about 10m (30ft) high, were used for, but the Kościuszko Mound was created to honour Kościuszko, and to emphasise the point it was partly built using earth from sites where Kościuszko's battles were fought.

Now it is a bit of a strange place. Part of the summit is occupied by an old and rather ugly Austrian fort dating from the 1840s, some of which is used by a radio station as their headquarters. They have named the small courtyard outside the entrance to the building Paul McCartney Square. The rest of the building is taken up by the Hotel Pod Kopcem and its restaurant (see p.129).

There's an excellent outdoor cafe with a good view over Kraków. You can pay to get into a small museum housed in a neo-Gothic chapel, where Kościuszko is reverentially remembered, which also gives access to a viewpoint at the very top of the mound, reached by a spiral path that circles up it.

To Get There

Take bus number 100 from Salwator, the tram terminus outside the Norbertanek monastery on Kościuszki Street, on the north bank of the river 1200m west of the castle, or pick it up from where it starts, at Rondo Grunwaldzkie, across the river from Wawel; or take the opportunity for a pleasant walk to reach the mound – it takes 40 to 50 minutes from the city centre, along Tadeusza Kościuski and then right up św. Bronisławy, just after you pass the monastery. The last part of the walk is through shady woodlands and meadows where you can see deer, and is a very popular Sunday stroll. The walk also runs past the *Cmentarz Salwator*, one of the largest cemeteries in Kraków, which like all the city's cemeteries is very busy on All Saints Day (November 1st; see p.137).

souvenir to take home with them.

From the bus and rail station it's a ten minute walk across an area of parkland to the Old Town, marked by a slight rise in the land and reached by short flights of steps that bring visitors to the back of the onion-domed **Church of the Presentation of the Virgin Mary** *(Kościół Ofiarowania NMP)*. The focal point of this fairly unremarkable Baroque church (built 1791-8 with the tower added in the nineteenth century) is a side chapel containing a nineteenth century image of the Virgin Mary in front of which the young Karol used to pray regularly. A stall in the church sells Pope-oriented souvenirs, while images and photographs of the town's adored son adorn many of the walls. Outside, the church fronts one side of the attractive town square, pl.Jana Pawla II, whose spaciousness and planted flowerbeds make it ideal for a drink or meal during summer at one of the open-air restaurants. Behind the church the upper floor of the former Town Hall has been converted into the **town museum** (Muzeum Miejskie, open daily) where the history of the town (which rose to prominence in the nineteenth century as a district capital and a barracks for the Austro-Hungarian army) is traced through old photographs and documents. The ground floor of this building houses a useful and knowledgeable **tourist office**. At ul.Kościelna 7, virtually opposite the museum, the house (**casa natale**) in which Karol Wojtyła was born on May 18th 1920 has been turned into a museum of his life, crammed with photographs and other memorabilia, which show that in his youth the future pontiff was a keen skier and walker, acted in school plays and regularly played football. (Open May-September 9am-1pm and 2-6pm; October-April 9am-noon, 1-6pm)

Beyond these three sites there is little to do in Wadowice beside people-watching in the main square or seek out a restaurant or café selling a local speciality called *Kremówka Wadaowicka*, a slice of creamy custard. For those who want to see more, a twenty minute stroll from the main square south along al Matki Bozej Fatimskiej will bring you to the Kościół św.Piotra Apostola (**Church of St Peter the Apostle**). This strikingly modern church was built to give thanks for the Pope surviving an assassination attempt in May 1981. Its architects, Ewa Węcławowicz-Gyurkovich and Jacek Gyurkovich, intended its sense of light to portray the triumph of good over evil.

Wadowice is linked to Kraków by regular bus services, which leave from either of the two terminals in Kraków (see p.152-53) and take around 70 minutes. Trains between the two centres are less frequent and take rather longer.

Częstochowa

Situated 130km northwest of Kraków, **Częstochowa** is one of the world's greatest sites of Catholic pilgrimage, receiving around four million pilgrims every year. Rising on a low hill in the midsts of this rather drab industrial city, a monastery complex known as Jasna Góra ("Luminous Hill"), whose origins date back to the fourteenth century, house a much-venerated icon: a painting of the Virgin Mary known as the

"Black Madonna". The site is always busy with worshippers, but on major Marian festival days (May 3, August 26, September 8 and December 8) the town often plays host to up to a million pilgrims, and during the Feast of the Assumption (August 15), the principal feast day devoted to the Virgin Mary, thousands make a pilgrimage here on foot from places as far afield as Warsaw.

Those who come to Częstochowa by train or bus (see p.110) will enter the monastery by the eastern (main)

Karol Wojtyła: Pope John Paul II

Karol Wojtyła spent the first eighteen years of his life in Wadowice. In his youth he was keen on football, skiing, poetry and acting. At the time of the outbreak of World War Two he was a student of Polish literature at the Jagiellonian University in Kraków. When the University was closed by the Nazis Wojtyła was sent to work in a stone quarry as part of a gang of forced labourers. However, he continued his studies in secret, and was also active in the underground Rhapsody Theatre. In 1942 he began studying (illegally) for the priesthood in Kraków; when the war was over he taught at the re-opened Jagiellonian University and in the Polish city of Lublin. In 1963 he became Archbishop of Kraków and was made a cardinal three years later. In 1978 he was elected pope – the first non-Italian to hold the position since 1522.

Although he was a controversial figure as pope – particularly in his traditionalist stance on matters like abortion and contraception, which has angered many liberals in the Catholic church – Wojtyła was an enormously important figure in Poland's recent history. His anti-Communist stance was an acute embarrassment to the former regime, and as Pope John Paul II he became a focal point for the anti-government demonstrations of the 1980s; the eventual success of the free trade union movement *Solidarity* was due partly to the presence of such a crucial figure of the international stage, which meant that Poland could rarely be ignored or isolated from the world's gaze, even during the darkest days of martial law (1981-83).

Poland is a deeply Catholic country and Pope John Paul II has a place in Polish hearts occupied by no other person in history. His visit to Poland in 1979 drew the largest gathering the country has ever seen, fomenting political opinion at the time. The attempt made on his life in 1981 drew nearly a million people onto the streets of Kraków, all dressed in white, in a peaceful demonstration of solidarity that became known as the "White March". In 1991 he celebrated Mass in the Rynek Główny from an open-air altar built outside St Mary's Church. When he died, on April 2 2005, he was deeply mourned by the Polish people, who will continue to celebrate his legacy for a long time to come.

entrance, a paved way leading through trees at the foot of which is a statue commemorating **Jerzy Popiełuszko**. He was the radical priest whose support of the Polish free Trade Union, Solidarity, led to his murder by the Polish state security forces in 1984; he is now revered as something of a national martyr. From here the paved way leads up to a vast grassy space where the faithful gather during major festivals. **Pope John Paul II** made six pilgrimages here during his papacy, each time drawing crowds of hundreds of thousands of people to this spot.

From the grassy plain where the faithful gather the **monastery complex** itself is accessed through gateways that cut through the massive defensive walls. The monastery is always humming with visitors, priests, nuns (who run the information office and the museums) and pilgrims, many of whom stay in the purpose-built pilgrims' hostels that surround the site. The **Chapel of the Miraculous Image**, reached by passing through the larger and adjacent early eighteenth century **Basilica**, is the focal point of the complex; the actual "Black Madonna" sits above a raised altar in a Gothic chapel whose walls are crammed with votive offerings and with crutches thrown away by those who have been cured by coming here. For some of the time the image is covered by an ornate eighteenth century silver screen, which is raised on occasions (usually at 1.30pm) to a

The spiritual heart of Poland

The first defences around the Jasna Góra monastery were built in late medieval times. The defences were first put to the test in 1655 when they helped the monastery withstand a six-week siege by the Swedish army. At that time Sweden was an emerging European power, expanding its empire to encompass the lands on the south side of the Baltic. When Jasna Góra was besieged, Poznań, Kraków and Warsaw were already in Swedish hands. But four thousand well-trained Swedish troops failed to dislodge the monastery's two hundred and fifty defenders, a triumphant victory that helped turn the monastery into something of a symbol of Polish nationalism. In 1770, by which time the Black Madonna had been crowned "Queen of Poland", the place once again withstood a fierce siege, this time by the Russians. To this day the monastery is one of the most powerful symbols of Polish nationhood and freedom, in addition to providing the most tangible evidence for the influence and strength of the Catholic Church in this country. This was made clear in September 1946 when, in the presence of half a million worshippers at Jasna Góra, the Primate of Poland consecrated the country to the Immaculate Heart of St Mary, thanking her for saving the nation from the Nazis. In June 1983 Pope John Paul II preached here on the theme of freedom during the darkest days of Communism and martial law. His donations to the monastery included the blood-soaked belt of the cassock he had been wearing during the assassination attempt made on his life two years previously. John Paul II's devotion to this shrine helped keep Poland in the international spotlight during the troubled years of the 1980s and was very unsettling for the country's Communist rulers at the time. In 1999, on John Paul's last visit, he prayed here with the words "Mother of Jasna Góra, Queen of Poland, please take my whole nation into your maternal heart."

The Black Madonna

The history of this famous painting, which depicts a solemn-looking Virgin holding the Christ Child with his hand raised in blessing, is rather obscure. What is certain is that it was a donation from King Wadisław II, who founded the monastery in 1382, and introduced the first monks, who were members of a Pauline community in Hungary. According to tradition the image was painted by the Apostle St Luke onto a wooden tabletop taken from the house of the Holy Family in Nazareth (another image of Mary painted by Luke is housed in a church in Bologna); however scientific tests reveal the icon to date from between the sixth and ninth centuries, making it a Byzantine-era icon, and in fact the image may be a painted-over copy of the original, which was the victim of a theft by followers of the Czech religious reformer John Huss in 1430. Events surrounding this theft have also endowed the painting with religious significance: the thieves apparently found the image grew increasingly heavy as they carried it away, and, in anger, they slashed it, after which real blood began seeping from the wounds. To this day the Virgin's cheek is still cut by two distinct gashes (the dark colouring of the face, which gives the image its name, is thought to be caused by age and centuries of exposure to incense).

glorious fanfare of trumpets and a roll of drums played by an (unseen) band made up of priests. This is a fascinating ceremony, and worth watching (the information office will be able to supply details of the times when the screen is raised). The Virgin and Child wear jewel-encrusted robes that are changed at regular intervals, so even when the screen is raised all that is visible of the icon are the hands and faces.

Three separate museums can be found within the monastery complex. The **Treasury** houses a valuable collection of altar pieces and liturgical vestments, and can get crowded when the monastery is busy with visitors. Most of the items here are gifts made to the monastery: the earliest gifts date from the sixteenth century, whereas the most recent is a chalice given by the French episcopate in 1982. (Close by, in the shadow of the Basilica, the distinctive chapel that fronts a secluded arcaded courtyard is the twentieth-century **Chapel of the Last Supper**.) The **Muzeum Sześçsetlecia** is the Six Hundredth Anniversary Museum, established in 1982, which tells some of the history of the monastery. Exhibits include various Bibles printed by the monastic printing house, and the Nobel Peace Prize awarded in 1983 to Lech Wałęsa, the leader of the free Trade Union Solidarity, whose name was rarely far from the news during the 1980s and who chose to donate the award to the monastery. In the **Arsenal** you can see displays relating to the military defences of the monastery.

Other places to see in the monastery complex include the **Stations of the Cross**, created between 1900 and 1913 by the architect Stefan Szyller and the sculptor Pius Welonski, which stand on a series of artificial rocks just beyond the monastery walls (clearly signposted); and the **Knights Hall** (adorned with paintings and flags) and **Refectory** (boasting an amazing set of seventeenth century ceiling frescoes), the monastery's most sumptuously-decorated public rooms, which are usually off-limits to visitors (but ask

Getting to Częstochowa

Częstochowa takes two hours to reach by train from Kraków, making the place a viable day-trip; the line runs through a pleasant landscape of fields, farms, villages and undulating countryside before reaching the grey industrial suburbs of Częstochowa itself. From the railway station, visitors should follow the pictorial signs showing the church, heading out over the station concourse and across the tram lines to al.Wolności; turning right along this street, then left onto al.Najświętszej Marii Panny (al NMP) just after the McDonalds, will bring you in sight of the monastery with its distinctive tall spire (soaring to 106m and visible from miles around). It's a walk of around 20-30 minutes from the station to the monastery; on al NMP you will pass St James' Church (on the right), a former Russian Orthodox Church dating from the time when this town formed the westernmost extent of the Russian Empire; and, further on, on the left, a tourist office at number 65.

Buses also link Kraków with Częstochowa and are marginally slower than trains. The bus station is on al. Wolności, next to the railway station. Those driving to Częstochowa, or coming by coach on one of the tours offered by hotels and tourist offices in Kraków, will find themselves parking in the huge car parks adjoining the monastery's western (back) entrance.

at the information office if you really want to look round them). Finally, the climb up to the viewing gallery in the **bell tower** is well worth the effort.The fabulous view encompasses the grey housing blocks and wide, windswept boulevards of the city – once a model Socialist industrial centre – which give way to the rather featureless countryside beyond. From the bell tower it is also possible to appreciate the size of the monastery, and the massiveness of its walls, most of which date from 1843 and were built on the orders of Tsar Nicholas I when this part of Poland was in Russian hands.

Zakopane

Eighty kilometers south of Kraków the gently wooded hills of southern Poland give way to a range of soaring mountains that stretch in an east-west arc along the border with Slovakia. These are the **Tatras** (*Tatry* in Polish), a spectacular Alpine range whose highest peak (Gerlachovsky Stit, situated just over the border) rises to a height of 2655m. The Tatras are part of the Carpathians, the arc of mountains that stretch through Eastern Europe covering parts of Slovakia, Poland, Hungary and Romania. The principal mountain resort in the Polish Tatras is **Zakopane**, a two-hour journey by road from Kraków and easily visited from there in a day trip. The resort boasts many opportunities for skiers in winter and walkers in summer, as well as a cable car (see p.113), a funicular railway and all the familiar trappings of a European ski resort. The town also has an important place in the cultural history of Poland as during the early decades of the twentieth century it was the haunt of a bohemian community of avant-garde writers and artists. However, Zakopane has a significant drawback too – three million visitors

From farming community to mountain resort

The small farming community of Zakopane began to develop as a mountain resort in the 1870s, when many people from the cities came here to seek a fresh-air cure for their tuberculosis. Then came the Kraków-based writers and artists, who began taking over the place during the summer months towards the end of the nineteenth century. These colourful intellectuals were part of an artistic movement known as Young Poland *(Młoda Polska)* which blended contemporary European styles such as art nouveau with a nostalgic, romantic yearning for Poland's traditional past. One of the most noted members of this group was Stanislaw Witkiewicz (1851-1915), a painter and architect who developed a distinctive style of architecture characterized by steep roofs, all-wood construction and a deliberate nod towards traditional forms of local rustic architecture. He built a number of large Alpine-style chalets in the Zakopane region and decorated them with motifs borrowed from houses built by the local peasants. Meanwhile other artists and composers who were part of the same movement sought inspiration for their work in the local craft-making and musical traditions.

After the end of the First World War, however, a new breed of visitor began to jostle for space in Zakopane with the artists and intellectuals: these were the tourists, who started coming to the town in droves to ski in winter and hike in the surrounding mountains in summer. The first skiers arrived in 1906; during the 1930s the first ski-lifts were built, and after World War Two skiing became the town's main form of income. However those who come here to ski today will find the runs here short and rather busy compared to other European skiing centres.

annually come here to spend time in the mountains, and the place can get uncomfortably crowded in summer and at weekends throughout the year.

From the bus and railway stations it's a ten minute walk along ul.Kościuszki, past the ostentatious Grand Hotel and the tourist information office, to **ul.Krupówki**, the town's pedestrianized and gently sloping main street, which is lined with a motley collection of souvenir shops, hotels and restaurants. Turning right along this street will bring you to the town's main sights. The **Muzeum Tatrzanskie**, set back a little from the road in a two-storey nineteenth century house, tells the story of the Polish Tatras through re-created interiors of peasant houses, examples of traditional costumes worn by mountain folk, and the photographs of Titus Chałubinski, a local doctor who championed the town's qualities as a health centre. Unfortunately labelling is mostly only in Polish throughout the museum. Further on along ul.Krupówki the attractive Parish Church appears on the right, set on a slight rise; turning left immediately after the church, along ul.Kościelska, brings you to the wooden **Church of St Clement** *(Kościół św.Klimenta)* a mid nineteenth century church built in the rustic, traditional style of the Carpathians. Inside the decoration includes devotional paintings on glass, a local folk art tradition, while above the altar is an image of the Black Madonna of Częstochowa (see p.109). In the cemetery adjacent to the church there are graves of a number of intellectuals associated with Zakopane during the last century, including Stanisław Witkiewicz (see above), whose grave consists of a wooden totem

Getting to Zakopane

Although it is perfectly possible to drive by car from Kraków to Zakopane, the traffic jams and problems with parking in the resort will lead to many visitors preferring to take the bus or train, particularly during the summer. Coaches leave Kraków's main bus station (see pp151-52) for Zakopane throughout the day and take just over two hours; the much slower trains takes anything up to four hours to grind their way through the pleasant countryside between the two centres.

pole with a statue of Christ set into a niche. Those interested in the work of this noted architect should continue along the road past the wooden church to the **Willa Koliba**. This building, which Witkiewicz designed, is now a museum dedicated to his work and to that of his son, Witkacy, a writer, artist and drug addict who committed suicide in 1939 at the height of his fame as one of Zakopane's most colourful intellectuals.

Back at the junction of streets just outside the Parish Church, the northward continuation of ul. Krupówki runs through an underpass that is the scene of a colourful **market**. Here it is possible to buy many specialities of this region, such as items of folk art, and sheepskin and woodwork products, including *kierpce* (traditional moccasins from the region) and *ciupagi* (traditional walking sticks with decorative handles); and *oscypek*, the locally-produced sheep's cheese whose methods of production is kept a closely-guarded secret, passed down from family to family through the generations. (The cheese is unpasteurized, which might make it illegal to import into countries such as the UK, and is usually sold from vendors in smoked, lozenge-shaped blocks.)

Heading through the underpass brings you to the lower station of a **funicular railway to Gubałówka Hill** (long queues possible at busy times). The train *(droga)*, hauled by ropes up a steeply-rising set of rails, will take you up to an altitude of 1120m and an excellent view of the Tatras (it's also possible to walk up on a track beside the railway). At the top, besides the view, is a predictable collection of restaurants and souvenir places, plus a toboggan run. As regards hikes, one place to aim for from here is the village of **Witów**, which takes around two hours to reach on foot and is linked by bus to Zakopane. Maps of the region are widely available in Zakopane and show the colour-coded walking tracks that criss-cross the hills and valleys.

Rafting along the River Dunajec

A trip by raft through the spectacular Dunajec Gorge *(Spływ Dunajcem)* forms a popular excursion for visitors who are in Kraków in the Summer. The gorge runs through a set of rugged limestone hills that form the heart of the **Pieniny** region. Once logs were floated downriver to paper mills, but since the 1830s the transport of tourists by raft through the picturesque scenery has been the principal form river activity. The raft trips begin from the small village of

The Cable Car to Kasprowy Wierch

Zakopane's biggest draw for visitors is a cable car which runs up to Kasprowy Wierch (1985m), a high ridge that marks the border with Slovakia. The lower terminus of the cable car is at Kuźnice, a hamlet around three kilometers from Zakopane. There are buses there from the railway station in Zakopane – or you can take a taxi. From the summit station there is a path back down to Kuźnice (two hours walking time) for those who do not want to ride back down in the cabins. The view from the top is of course fabulous – but it comes at a price. In summer the cable car is often booked solid (the Orbis office on ul. Krupowki in Zakopane can sell tickets) and it will be difficult to ride on the cable car unless you are staying in the town and so are able to book several days in advance (or come here on an organized coach tour from Kraków that includes a ride up on the cable car as part of the package). You are more likely to be able to ride up to Kasprowy Wierch if you are here on a weekday in the off-season, although at these times the cable car is sometimes closed for maintenance. If you manage to get a ride up, take warm clothing, as it can be very cold at the top, even if it is a warm in the valleys; and of course take adequate shoes and outdoor gear if you intend to do any walking.

Stromowce Kąty, twenty kilometers southeast of **Nowy Targ**, from where there are buses to both Stromowce Kąty and Kraków. The rafting season operates from May to October and each raft *(tratwa)* leaves as it fills up; you may have to queue at busy times (avoid making the trip at weekends if possible). Rafts carry ten people and two operators, often dressed in traditional and colourful local costumes. For much of the way the river forms an international border with Slovakia and you will see other rafts operated by Slovak firms plying the same route.

The three hour trip along the gently-flowing waters first runs southeast from Kąty past a monastery on the Slovak side, Cerveny Klastor, and then heads northeast for a while; after passing the Ostra Skała (the Sharp Rock) there is a sharp right-turn into the narrowest part of the gorge, after which the river winds and twists before the rafts end up at a popular spa and tourist centre called **Szczawnica**. From here there are frequent free buses, run by the rafting company, back to Stomowce Katy. Szczawnica also boasts a small *pijalnia* where you can sample the local curative waters, and a chairlift that runs up to the summit of **Góra Palenica** (722m) from where there are some good views over the surrounding countryside.

Tourist offices in Kraków offer day-trips to the Pieniny which include a raft trip and a visit to the thirteenth century **Czorsztyn Castle** and its fourteenth century counterpart **Niedzica Castle**, both built as strategic strongholds to defend the trade routes into Hungary that once ran along the gorge. The former castle was destroyed in a peasant uprising and by a fire that resulted from a lightning strike in the 1790s, and is now in ruins, although the restored towers and battlements offer some superlative views; the latter houses a hotel and a museum that contains a number of folk costumes from the local area. Both castles overlook **Lake Czorsztyńskie**, situated to the west of Stromowce Kąty.

5. Auschwitz-Birkenau

Auschwitz-Birkenau - Some History

After the defeat and occupation of Poland by Nazi Germany in September 1939, the town of Oświęcim, 50km (30 miles) west of Kraków, became part of the Third Reich and was renamed Auschwitz. Soon afterwards the disused former barracks of the Polish army at Auschwitz was turned into a concentration camp for Polish political prisoners. The choice was based on remoteness, the available room for expansion, and proximity to an important railway junction.

The fearsome figure of Rudolf Hoss was appointed the first camp commandant, and the first prisoners entered the camp on June 14, 1940. They were mainly Polish Jews, and their imprisonment was part of Hitler's plan to subjugate, and eventually obliterate, the Polish nation.

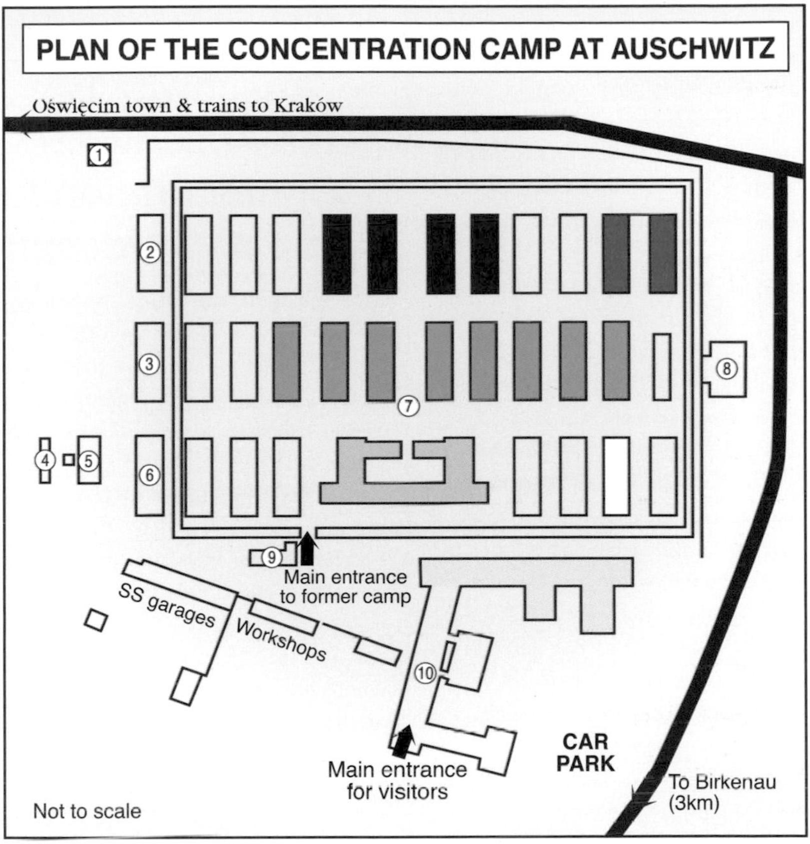

Opposite: The main gate at Auschwitz

PLAN OF THE CONCENTRATION CAMP AT AUSCHWITZ

Oświęcim town & trains to Kraków

① ② ③ ④ ⑤ ⑥ ⑦ ⑧ ⑨

Main entrance to former camp

SS garages

Workshops

⑩

Main entrance for visitors

CAR PARK

To Birkenau (3km)

Not to scale

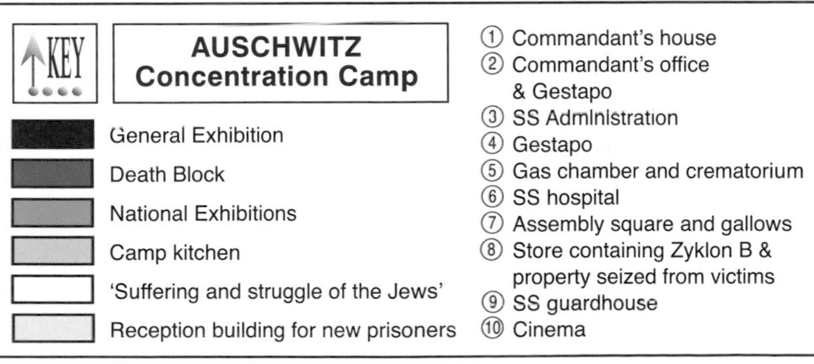

The workforce of prisoners gradually extended the camp over the following months and by 1942 the camp at Auschwitz housed as many as 20,000 people at any one time. In 1942 Heinrich Himmler, the architect of the Nazi's "final solution" to obliterate European Jewry, decided that Auschwitz should become a mass killing centre for Jews. This led to the construction of a second camp, Auschwitz II, located close by at Birkenau and established specifically for the purpose of exterminating Jews from all over Europe. Auschwitz I was a concentration camp, rather than an extermination camp, although many tens of thousands of people died here. Death came through random individual execution, and mass executions; through being worked too hard and fed too little; and through the incredibly unsanitary conditions of the camps, which led to the easy spread of infectious, fatal diseases. It was in Auschwitz I that Josef Mengele, the chief Nazi physician, carried out his experiments on prisoners, most notoriously on groups of twins.

In addition a third camp, Auschwitz III, was established in 1942 to house prisoners who worked under terrible conditions in the German chemical works run by IG Farben in Monowice, close by. Other steelworks, mines and factories in the area also supported further camps, using prisoners as slave labour.

From 1940 to 1945, when Auschwitz-Birkenau was liberated by advancing Soviet forces, between 1.5 and 2 million people died in the three camps here (the vast majority in Birkenau) and in the associated smaller camps in the surrounding area. Estimates of deaths are 75,000 Poles, 21,000 gypsies, 15,000 Soviet Prisoners of War, and 960,000 Jews.

Auschwitz I: the Auschwitz Concentration Camp at Oświęcim

The **modern entrance building**, incorporating part of the former reception building for new prisoners, includes a café, bookshop, information centre, exchange office and a **cinema** which is the best starting point for a visit. The film shown includes harrowing footage taken by the Soviet authorities who liberated the camp in May 1945, and is exhibited in English daily at 11am. Many have commented that it is inappropriate for the place where prisoners were shaved, robbed of their possessions, tattooed with a number and disinfected, to be full now of visitors buying snacks and using the toilets: that the place of initiation for prisoners is now the place of initiation for tourists. In fact the whole business of "tourist Auschwitz" may leave many visitors to the site feeling uncomfortable.

Beyond it is the camp proper, which you enter through the **main gates** carrying the words *Arbeit Macht Frei*, a cynical German exaltation to prisoners that "Work brings Freedom". Prisoners would pass through this gate every day on their way to work in the mines and factories of the surrounding area. Just inside the gate on the right is the camp kitchen where the camp orchestra

– made up of prisoners – would play stirring march tunes as the prisoners entered or left the camp or assembled for counting by the SS.

The bulk of the camp consists of blocks of prison cells, some of which are empty, others which have been given over to exhibitions of life in the camp and of the people brought to live and work here. The brick buildings are linked by avenues lined with trees, lending the place a stark, harsh atmosphere in winter and a sombre, gloomy one in summer. Throughout most of the site there are excellent and informative **information boards** in Polish, English and Hebrew, which means those who come here independently can get the most out of their visit (the same applies to Birkenau).

There are seven blocks given over to '**national exhibitions'** covering the fates of prisoners brought here from the USSR, Poland, Czechoslovakia, Yugoslavia / Austria, Hungary, France / Belgium and Italy / Holland. The eighth and most poignant is that devoted to the **Jews** who suffered here and at Birkenau. Furthest from the entrance gateway are a number of blocks given over to more general exhibitions – everyday lives of prisoners, living and sanitary conditions, and so on. The blocks serve as both reminders of, and memorials to, those who were imprisoned here, with much use made of photos, documents and (in the block devoted to the Jews) brief video shows.

Block 11 was known as the 'Death Block' and has been left largely as it was. Isolated from the rest of the camp, the first room you see in it was the office where the Gestapo police court met to issue death sentences to prisoners, sometimes more than a hundred in the space of a three hour sitting. Beyond it are cells for condemned prisoners, and bathrooms where prisoners were made to undress before being taken out and shot against the notorious 'execution wall' in the yard outside. The wooden blinds which cover the windows of the neighbouring block were there to stop people watching executions.

The gallows you can see in Block 11 were mobile and often used for public hangings of prisoners. It was also here that the SS punished prisoners for a whole host of crimes – working too slowly, picking apples, relieving themselves during work periods – by a number of methods, including flogging, confinement in cells, or hanging from the stake by the hands; you can see the original instruments used for these purposes.

In the cellar downstairs the first experiments with the gas Zyklon B were carried out in September 1941, when 600 Soviet Prisoners of War and 250 patients from the camp hospital were murdered, to test the efficiency of the gas later used to such devastating effect in Birkenau. The cells down here were used for prisoners who had been sentenced to death by starvation (the penalty for aiding an escape); a dark room, completely sealed, where prisoners died from suffocation; and other cells, including those on whose walls are drawings made by former inmates. One room is a shrine to the Polish-Catholic martyr Father Maksymilian Kolbe, canonized in 1982, who chose to die in the place of a man due to be executed. Upstairs in this block there is an exhibition commemorating the resistance movement which somehow emerged, despite the prospect of such harsh retributions on the part of the German authorities if perpetrators were ever discovered.

Over in the other part of the camp, the **crematorium** was situated immediately outside the main fence of the camp. Inside the entrance is the set of gallows used to hang Rudolf Hoss, the first camp commandant, on April 16th 1947. The largest room in the crematorium itself was converted into a temporary gas chamber where Jews and Soviet POWs were killed before the larger gas chambers at Birkenau were built. The ovens, designed by the German firm of *Topf und Sohne*, could dispose of 350 bodies per day. What you see now are reconstructions built by the museum in the late 1940s and based on the machines found at Birkenau, using some of the original metal parts.

Auschwitz II: the Birkenau Death Camp at Brzezinka

Birkenau was where the killing happened, on a vast and horrible scale. Thousands died at Auschwitz I, but well over a million people – and the actual number is not certain – died at Birkenau, the vast majority of them Jews, who were brought here from all over Europe from 1942 to 1944. The camp covers a vast area – 175 hectares (425 acres) – and the visitor's initial impression is of the sheer extent of the place. To walk around the site, from the main gates to the International Monument and then round the eastern edge of the site to the former Commandant's office, takes well over an hour.

The **main gates**, a familiar and iconic image of the Holocaust, remain intact: it was through these that the

Auschwitz

trains of cattle trucks full of Jews from all parts of Europe entered the camp. Nowadays you can get a good appreciation of the size and layout of the camp from the upstairs room of the gatehouse. But most of the rest of the buildings were burned or destroyed by the Nazis before the Russian army got here, in a hasty attempt to cover up one of the worst crimes against humanity ever conceived. All that remains of many of the former barracks (which were made of wood) are the brick chimneys, part of the rudimentary heating systems which were installed in them. Unlike Auschwitz I, there is no shop, cafe or exhibition space – indeed there are few visitors here; what there is, most of all, is silence.

The three hundred buildings here were barracks for prisoners, built mostly of wood on mud, without foundations or floors, and with brick chimneys leading from stoves which were supposed to provide some heat. In the **barracks that remain** (there are some brick ones over to the left after you enter the site, halfway along the rail tracks, and some other wooden ones which have been reconstructed immediately to the right of the entrance gate) you can see the conditions in which people were kept: wooden slats for bunks, swampy mud for a floor, the whole thing conceived with an unimaginable contempt for the prisoners who were brought here to die. The total number of men and women living in Birkenau reached a peak of 100,000 in August 1944: the place swarmed with rats and disease.

From the spring of 1942 Jews were brought here to be gassed, first from Poland, then from other parts of occupied Europe, from as far afield as Greece and Scandinavia. Those who came here were promised a new life under the Nazis, working in factories and farms vacated by Poles. The reality, of course, was different: when trains pulled up at the unloading ramps, SS men allocated about 70 per cent of prisoners (children, the old and the ill) for immediate gassing, whilst the rest were sent to work and live in camp.

Most got ill within a few months and they, in turn, would go to the gas chambers. Those selected to be killed would be told to undress and were given a towel and some soap, and were promised a shower. They were herded, two thousand at a time, to buildings at the end of the platform, where they would be killed by SS men pouring crystals of the toxic gas Zyklon B through slats in the ceiling.

The crematoria, which worked continuously, night and day, for three years, were next door. Zyklon B was devised specifically for the purpose of mass ex-termination (its crystals formed cyanide when they came into contact with air) and was manufactured by a German chemical plant in Hamburg. Its inventor, Dr Bruno Tesch, was executed for war crimes after being tried at Nuremberg.

The remains of the **crematoria** and gas chambers are still at the end of the platform, unstable, weed-infested and untouched since they were blown up by the SS in 1945. There's a pond where the ashes were thrown; and between the ruins of Crematoria II and III is **the International Monument to the Victims of Fascism**, unveiled in April

The Final Solution

Adolf Hitler's hatred of Jews is supposed to have emerged from his experiences in Vienna before the First World War when, as a struggling painter and decorator, he observed the large Jewish minority there and became a close follower of the city's anti-Semitic mayor, Karl Luger. By the time he fought in World War I he had assimilated the ideas of right-wing Bavarian extremists, and he was convinced that Germany's defeat in 1918 was a result of betrayal by Jewish and Marxist influences.

The goal of creating a supreme 'Aryan' race formed the core of Nazi policy as formulated during the 1920s, when Hitler, imprisoned after a failed coup (the Munich 'beer hall Putsch'), dictated his book *Mein Kampf* to his secretary Rudolf Hess. The book outlined Hitler's anti-Semitic prejudice and his hopes for the rekindling of German national pride after the 1918 defeat.

In 1933 Hitler assumed the Chancellorship of Germany and Jews became a specific target of oppression. Their persecution was enshrined in law and on 15th September 1935 German Jews were deprived of full German citizenship under the so-called 'Nuremberg Laws'. In November 1938, *Kristallnacht* saw the government-sponsored destruction of Jewish homes, synagogues and businesses. As the Third Reich expanded, the Nazi dream of creating a racially pure European Empire led to mass killings (mainly by execution squads) of over one million Jews in newly conquered areas of Europe between June and November 1941.

The 'Final Solution' was devised – with Hitler's support –by Heinrich Himmler, German Interior Minister and head of the *Schutzstaffel* (the SS: highly disciplined political soldiers), and his deputy Reinhard Heydrich, at a conference held in the Berlin suburb of Wannsee in January 1942. Himmler was passionate about his proposed extermination of Jews from Europe, "a page of glory in our history which has never been written and will never be written", he told his deputies.

Since the Nazi occupation of Poland in 1939, Jews had been forced to

1967. Beyond here are the clutches of beech trees which give the area its name in Polish (*Brzezinka* means "beech forest"); and just beyond these, the fields and farmhouses of rural Poland.

Oświęcim Town

Most visitors to Auschwitz-Birkenau are unlikely to see much of Oświęcim town, which lies 2km east of the concentration camp and railway station, across the river. Before the Holocaust, around seven thousand of the town's twelve thousand inhabitants were Jewish; its kosher vodka distillery was well-known throughout central Europe. The main draw here today is the **Jewish Centre** *(Centrum Żydowskie w Oświęcimiu)* on pl.ks.Jana Skarbka 3 (open daily except Saturdays and Jewish holidays). In the restored prayer hall of this former synagogue you can see a *bimah* (pulpit); upstairs there is live in tightly-controlled and defined ghettos in Warsaw, Kraków and other cities, and rounding them up for institutionalised massacre was a relatively straightforward task. Later, Jews from occupied France, Belgium, Greece, The Netherlands, Bohemia, Moravia and Russia were sent *en masse* to the 20 extermination camps where mass killings took place from the spring of 1942 onwards.

Extermination camps were established in Poland at Sztutowo (near Gdańsk), Treblinka and Sobibór (in north-eastern Poland) and Birkenau, Majdanek, Bełżec and Chełmno Nad Nerem (Cumhof) (in the south-east). Sobibór, Treblinka and Bełżec were destroyed by the Nazis in 1943 after 1.8 million people, mostly Jews, with smaller numbers of gentile Poles and Gypsies, had been murdered in their gas chambers.

The liberation in 1945 of Sztutowo, Birkenau and Cumhof, only a short time after these camps had ceased killing operations (and were still full of starving prisoners) allowed the world to see the full horrors of Himmler's solution to the "Jewish problem". Of all the camps, Birkenau killed the most. As late as the summer of 1944, as German military forces faced up to defeat on most of the fighting fronts, 450,000 Hungarian Jews were gassed here, the last of the big 'national' contingents of European Jewry to face the Nazi killing machine.

Nazi authority was underpinned by systemised massacre. Ruthless barbarism and the machinery that went with it were its hallmark and its most notorious legacy to the world. In total, around six million Jews died in the Holocaust; around one million others – Slavs, Gypsies (Romanies), homosexuals, Communists, Soviets, incurable invalids – were also killed, regarded by the Nazis as *Untermensch* – "subhumans".

Himmler, who would have been tried at Nuremberg after the war (as were many of his associates who perpetrated the 'Final Solution') took poison after being captured by the Allies at Luneberg; he was one of the last people to see Hitler alive in the Berlin bunker. Heydrich, who had been made head of the Protectorate of Bohemia and Moravia, was assassinated in Prague in 1942 by Czech freedom fighters.

a photographic exhibition of prewar Jewish life in the town, concentrating on mundane activities such as football matches and day-to-day life – a life that was wholly obliterated in 1941.

Auschwitz-Birkenau today

Since 1945 Auschwitz-Birkenau has been at the centre of struggles between Polish Catholics and Communists, and the Polish and global Jewish communities, as to what exactly the place stands for.

In the years following the end of the War, during the establishment of a Communist government in Poland, the camps were considered more of a memorial to the butchery of fascism and the attempts of Germany to obliterate Poland, than the location for the proposed extermination of Jews. This

Practical Information for visitors to

The former concentration camp of Auschwitz is located in the industrial town of Oświęcim, 50km (30 miles) due west of Kraków. Birkenau camp is 3km (2 miles) from the Auschwitz camp in the small village of Brzezinka.

By Car

A straightforward route on the A4 motorway past Balice airport (direction Katowice). Oświęcim is 18km (11 miles) from a signposted junction; follow signs for "Auschwitz: Muzeum", 45 – 60 minutes travelling time. Addresses of car rental offices in Kraków are given on page 133.

By Train

The Orbis state travel office on Rynek Glowny will give you a list of train times from Kraków to Oświęcim and sells tickets. There are 16 trains a day, but some leave from Płaszów station in the southern suburbs of Kraków; the rest leave from Główny, the main station.

Most trains take around 90 minutes; the fastest trains are slightly quicker and require seat reservation. For information about tickets and types of train see p.151. From the station at Oświęcim it's a 20 minute walk (or a journey by local bus or taxi) to Auschwitz concentration camp (turn right after leaving the station).

Taxis and buses (the latter only April-September) also link Auschwitz and Birkenau camps, or you can walk the 3 km (2 miles) between them (it's well signposted).

By Bus

Buses are less convenient than trains and some do not stop in the centre of Oświęcim town. However, they are cheaper than trains and take 90 minutes. Orbis on Rynek Główny have lists of departure times. Buses leave from the main bus station, next to the railway station (see p.000).

is why, in Auschwitz I, memorials are arranged by nationality, with specific pavilions given over to citizens of what became Soviet bloc countries; in fact the section remembering Jews who died was closed from 1967 to 1978.

In 1979 Pope John Paul II visited Auschwitz and held a Papal mass in Birkenau on the railway platform where Jews had once been selected for the gas chambers. In 1984 a Carmelite nunnery was established just outside the perimeter walls of Auschwitz. Both these incidents were interpreted by the world Jewish community as an attempt by the Catholic church to use the memory of the Holocaust for its own ends. In the late 1980s Auschwitz was the scene for demonstrations by both Catholics and Jews, each angered by what they saw as the 'other side's' interpretation for their own ends of the memory of

By Organised Tour

Many hotels in Kraków run organised tours to the camps, which can be useful as long as you don't mind being constrained by pre-arranged arrival and departure times. Some tours will have guides; others just let you get on with things on your own. Tourist offices in the city also run tours – try some of the private tourist offices along Floriańska, in addition to the state-run office on Pawia.

Opening Times

Opening times are : 8am – 3pm (16 Dec – end Feb), 8am – 4pm (Mar and Nov 1 – Dec 15), 8am – 5pm (Apr and Oct), 8am – 6pm (May and Sep), 8am – 7pm (June, July, Aug).

The cinema in the Auschwitz museum shows a short documentary film in English daily at 11am. The museum authorities recommend, but do not enforce, a rule that children under the age of 14 do not visit Auschwitz-Birkenau. Entry is free to both camps.

Further Information

The State Museum of Oświęcim has its own publishing house, producing books and other materials in Polish, English and other languages. There is an excellent English-language guide in pamphlet form, Auschwitz-Birkenau Guidebook, published in 1997 and ideal for a day visit. Other books relate to the history of the camps, and the personal recollections of survivors. There is a museum shop at the visitors' entrance to the Auschwitz site.

what occurred here.

Since 1990 the new regime in Poland has been more willing to recognise that much of the site was specifically established as the principal centre for the carrying out of the 'final solution', acknowledging that the vast majority of victims were Jews from all over Europe. The cross erected in 1979 was moved to a site outside the camp and in 1993 the monastery was relocated to a site 1km

The rail gateway to Birkenau

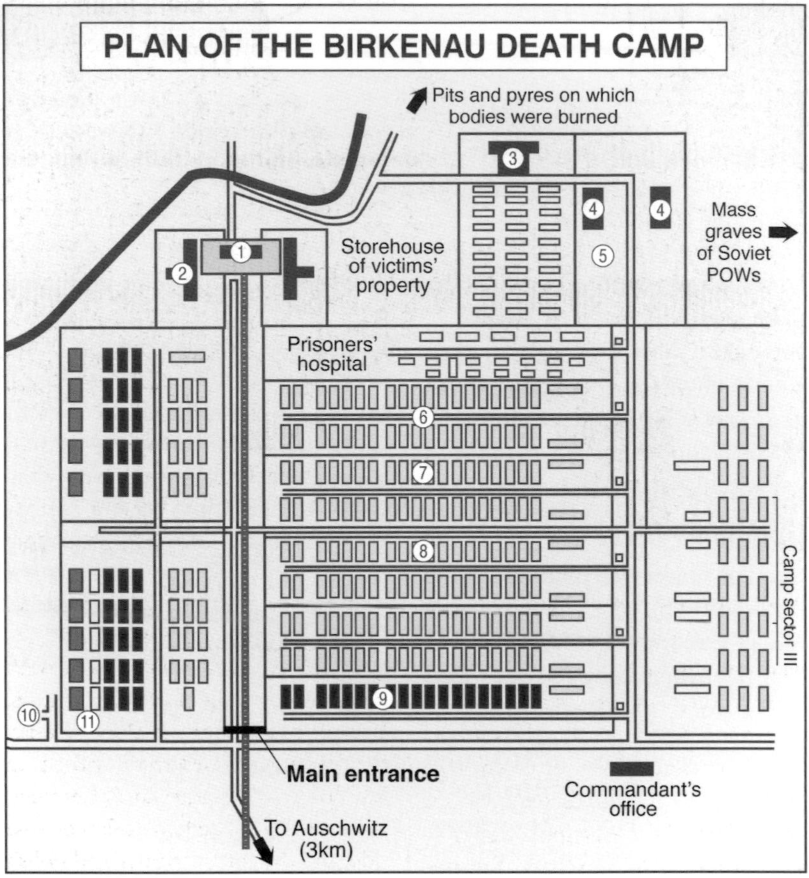

PLAN OF THE BIRKENAU DEATH CAMP

Pits and pyres on which bodies were burned

Mass graves of Soviet POWs

Storehouse of victims' property

Prisoners' hospital

Camp sector III

Main entrance

Commandant's office

To Auschwitz (3km)

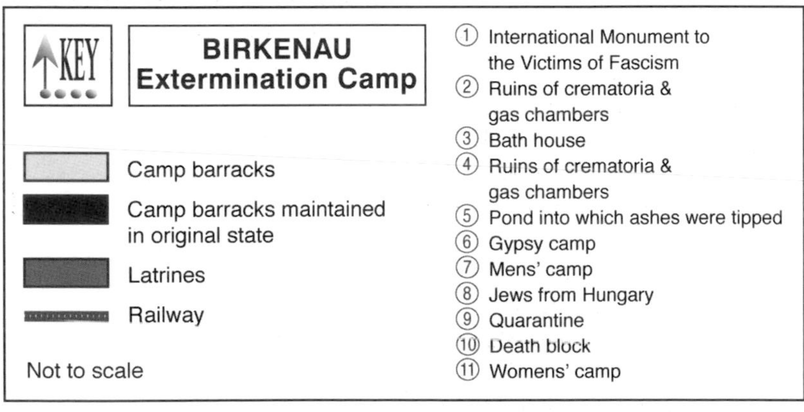

(600 yards) away from Auschwitz; for a while things looked as though they were calming down.

However in 1998, when suggestions were made that the cross might be taken down from its new site in deference to Jewish sensitivities, Polish Catholics leapt to its defence, and formed a 'Committee for the Defence of the Cross'.

Cardinal Josef Glemp, the Primate of Poland, said that the cross (and by extension the Auschwitz-Birkenau complex) stood as a reminder of Polish national suffering—thereby re-opening the old wounds of the 1980s. A Catholic extremist called Kazimierz Swinton, known for his anti-Semitic views, held a 42-day hunger strike under the cross; his supporters rapidly constructed 50 more crosses, an action condemned by Yad Vashem Holocaust Memorial officials in Jerusalem as "provocative".

The Polish government, not wishing to be embroiled any further in the conflict, has passed the responsibility over what to do with the crosses to the Catholic church. It would seem from these events that Auschwitz-Birkenau will be an ideological battleground between nationalist Poles and Catholics on one side, and the international and Polish Jewish communities on the other, for some time to come.

Accommodation

Kraków is becoming one of the most popular city destinations in Europe, and in summer, especially, you should book accommodation in advance to be sure of getting what you want. Doing this by fax, telephone, e-mail or post is straightforward; hotels are geared-up for English-speaking visitors and you'll usually find an English speaker on the end of the line if you phone in advance.

The 27 hotels, campsites and youth hostels described below give a representative selection of what's available. Although there are hotels (and motels) on the outskirts of town, these have not been included in the list below; most of the following establishments are all within easy walking distance of the centre (if they're not, that's mentioned in the description).

A number of good websites have information relating to hotels in Kraków. All these websites allow payment by credit card; sometimes the full hotel bill is paid in advance, at other times only a small part of it is paid and the balance must be settled at the hotel. Printed off vouchers sent by email must be presented at the hotel when you arrive. The cheapest hotels, along with hostels and campsites, are not included on these sites. However you can often pick up good discounts in expensive hotels on these sites, particularly in winter. Websites dealing with accommodation in Poland include www.visitpoland.com, www.polhotels.com and www.discover-poland.pl. Other sites such as www.expedia.co.uk deal with hotels around the world but have extensive listings for Kraków. It is also possible to book ther services such as flights or car hire on these sites.

Waweltour, located opposite the railway station at Pawia 8 and open 8am-7pm Mon-Fri and until 2pm on Sat (closed Sun), is the place to arrange private rooms in Kraków. A stay with a Polish family will be easily affordable, although you should look at a map carefully before you agree to a place as some addresses are miles out from the centre (although public transport links from the suburbs are excellent and very cheap). Their phone number is ☎(012) 422 1921 or 422 1640. During the summer private individuals also congregate here and outside the railway station, offering rooms to visitors; make sure you find out the exact price and location before accepting – and ideally look round it first. Some bargaining over the price may be possible. The tourist office keeps lists of hotels, although you are probably better off calling places direct. Agencies offering private apartments for visitors who wish to stay longer in Kraków include Old Town Apartments (☎ 022 820 93227, or 0871 733 3032 from the UK; (www.warsawhotel.com) and Janexim at number 4, ul.Karmelicka 11 (☎ 012) 429 1118; (www.krakowrooms.janexim.pl).

The following is a list of selected places to stay, graded in price from cheapest ($) to most expensive ($$$$). All hotels will have double and single rooms available, and some will have triples. Singles cost around 60-70% of the price you'll pay for a double room. In the winter many hotels reduce their prices, sometimes by as much as half, and there are good deals to be found on websites such as those listed above.

Krakowianka $

Żywiecka Boczna 2
☎ (012) 268 1135
This campsite with chalets is located 6km south of the town centre in the Borek Fałęcki district, 200m west of Zakopianska, the main road to Zakopane, along which run many tram and bus routes run into the centre. There are places for tents and caravans, with some chalet-bungalows on offer too, and three-bed rooms in a one-storey accommodation building. Situated close to woodland with a restaurant and an outdoor pool. Open May-Sep only.

Camping Krak $

Radzikowskiego 99
☎ (012) 637 2122
Huge campsite located 5km northwest of the city centre close to a busy roundabout, overlooked by the *Motel Krak*. Take bus 602 from the Polonia Hotel, close to the station, and change onto the 118 at Nowy Kleparz. Rooms available all year round. Camping only available May-Sep.

Strawberry Youth Hostel $

ul. Racławicka 9
☎ (012) 636 1500
One of a network of Central European hostels providing cheap accommodation in university dormitories to summer backpackers (there are others in Prague and Budapest). Most rooms sleep 2, 3 or 4, with showers along the corridor. They operate a free bus to the station (where they usually have a booth to attract newly-arrived travellers). Open July and August only. Ten minutes by tram from the centre, or a 30-minute walk.

Studencki Hotel Piast $

Piastowska 47
☎ (012) 637 4933
www.piast.bratniak.Kraków.pl
piast@bratniak.Kraków.pl
Huge block of student dormitories located north-west of the centre (15 minutes by tram; 45 minutes on foot). Bus 511 or 501 from the station stops outside. Singles, doubles and triples. Mainly operates in July and August, during the university holidays; some rooms may be available in term time at other times of the year too. The surrounding area is a lively student village, busy with Polish students in term time and language students from all over the world in the summer. Shared bathrooms. Big advantage – a laundry, for the use of guests and non-guests.

Hostel Rynek 7 $

Rynek Główny 7
☎ (012) 431 1698
email: hostel@hostelrynek7.pl
www.hostelrynek7.pl
Hostel in an unbeatable location on the main square; some rooms have views over it. Accommodation in dormitories with bunk beds. Bike rental and guided tours available; satellite TV and multi-lingual staff. Student discount.

Nathan's Villa $

św. Agnieszki 1
☎ 012 422 3435
www.nathansvilla.com
This busy, friendly backpackers' hostel is located 1km south of the main square, between Wawel Hill and the Kazimierz district, on a quiet side street that runs off the busy Stradomska. There are bunk beds in dormitories and common room facilities.

Hotel Retro $$

Barska 59
☎ (012) 266 0708
Cheap hotel located across the river from the castle; not an attractive part of town, but the views from some of the rooms are very nice. Recommended if you're looking for something more than a hostel at a very affordable price.

Hotel Korona $$

Kalwaryjska 9-15
☎ (012) 656 1566
An inauspicious location – above a row of shops on a main road – this is a cheap

hotel, charging only 140 zł for a double room with a bath. The rooms are fine, if rather spartan, and the location, on the south side of the Wisła, is well away from the most well-known parts of tourist Kraków – although a tram route running outside the hotel means that the centre is only around 20 minutes away. The hotel is part of the Korona Sports Club and there is a swimming pool, a gym and a sports hall that guests can use (see map p.82).

Hotel Pod Wawelem $$

Pl. Na Groblach 22 (on the corner with Powiśle)
☎ (012) 426 2626
www.hotelpodwawelem.pl
Small hotel located directly opposite Wawel Castle (of which there are outstanding views) with 47 comfortable rooms, all ensuite and with satellite TV. There's also a (rather drably furnished) restaurant on the ground floor. Advance booking recommended. (Formerly the Pensjonat Rycerska.)

Klezmer-Hois Hotel $$

Szeroka 6
☎/fax (012) 411 1622
klezmer-hois@klezmer-hois.Kraków.pl
www.klezmer.pl
Attractive hotel located in a refurbished ancient building which once housed a ritual bath of the Jewish Quarter (the columns are still visible). A twenty-minute walk or short tram ride from the centre of town, this is a characterful hotel, with very spacious rooms and an attractive downstairs coffee bar. Live evening folk music in the restaurant here and in the close-by *Ariel* and *Alef* restaurants.

Alef Hotel $$

Szeroka 17
☎/fax (012) 421 3870
alef@alef.pl
www.alef.pl
The *Alef* is actually better known as an excellent restaurant on the main square of the Jewish Quarter, serving really good non-kosher food and providing live entertainment most evenings (see p.145). Above the restaurant are five suites, furnished in turn-of-the-century style, making for an attractive, quiet and unusual place to stay in the city. There are no TVs in the rooms; the whole place is supposed to suggest a nostalgia for bygone days. The hotel is a twenty minute walk, or a short tram ride away, from the city centre.

Hotel Eden $$

ul. Ciemna 15
☎ (012) 430 6565
www.hoteleden.pl
Kraków's only Jewish hotel and the only place where you can eat genuine kosher food (though you need to order in advance). It also has a *mikvah*, a ritual bath house. All rooms have bathrooms and a satellite TV. Prices almost halve between November and April.

Hotel Fortuna $$$

Corner of Piłsudskiego and Czapskich
☎/fax (012) 422 3143
info@hotel-fortuna.com.pl
A ten minute walk from the main square (the route takes you through the university area and an attractive corner of the *Planty*), this is a recently-renovated hotel in an historic building, which was previously a college run by Piarist monks. Now there are spacious, well-appointed rooms set around attractive courtyards.

Hotel Wawel Tourist $$$

Poselska 22
☎ (012) 424 1300
fax (012) 422 0439
www.wawel-tourist.com.pl
Ideally situated on a very quiet street less than five minute's walk from the main square, this hotel, located in a renovated sixteenth century house, is friendlier and less impersonal than many in this category. Rooms are spacious, and with a certain amount of character, and the hotel has a bar and a restaurant offering traditional European cuisine.

Hotel Wyspiański PTTK $$$

Westerplatte 15
☎ (012) 422 9566
fax (012) 422 5719
wyspianski@janpol.com.pl
www.hotel-wyspianski.pl
Modern and bland, but cheap and central hotel, whose façade overlooks the *Planty*. A couple of minutes walk from the main square.

Polonia Hotel $$$

Basztowa 25
☎ (012) 422 1233;
fax (012) 422 1621
www.hotel-polonia.com
email: polonia@bci.Kraków.pl
Large, reasonably priced hotel in hard-to-beat location between the station and main square. Historic building which the Polonia hotel has occupied since 1917. Some of the rooms remain rather down-at-heal despite recent modernization; others have restored nineteenth century furnishings.

Hotel Europejski $$$

Lubicz 5
☎ (012) 423 2510
fax (012) 423 25 29
email: he@he.pl
Another hotel located close to the station; slightly more refined than others close by, with an elegant façade overlooking the main road and slightly old-fashioned rooms with parquet floors, some of which overlook the main courtyard. A walk of five minutes or so to the main square.

Hotel Warszawski $$$

Pawia 6
☎ (012) 424 2100
fax (012) 424 2200
Another reasonably priced hotel located near the station: an ancient and elegant building with a restored neo-classical façade which gives way to a very smart, if a little soulless, interior. A five minute walk from the centre of town.

Hotel Ester $$$

Szeroka 20
☎ (012) 429 1188
fax (012) 429 1233
biuro@hotel-ester.Krakow.pl
www.hotel-ester.Krakow.pl
Very well-appointed hotel, with spacious and attractive rooms, located on the main square of the Jewish Quarter, a twenty-minute walk or short tram ride from the centre of town. Less bland than other hotels in this category. Restaurant and bar serving international cuisine; characterful kosher restaurants with live folk music in the evenings very close by.

Hotel Pod Różą $$$

ul. Floriańska 14
☎ (012) 424 3300
fax (012) 424 3351
pod-roza@hotel.com.pl
Stylish, opulent, centuries-old hotel built around a central glassed-in courtyard and located right in the heart of town, on the main shopping street, barely a minute from St Mary's Church and the Rynek Główny. Of course, you pay for these advantages (see also p.39).

Pod Kopcem Hotel FM $$$

al. Waszyngtona
☎ (012) 427 0355
fax (012) 427 0101
Situated 3km (2 miles) west of the city centre in an old Austrian fort at the foot of the 300m (1000ft) high Kościuszko Mound; easy, direct bus links with city centre. Smart and very quiet, full of thick carpets and excellently-appointed rooms, with good views from some of the rooms that on a clear day can stretch as far as the High Tatras. Luxurious but slightly eccentric: the hotel occupies the same building as the national radio station RMF FM and numbers and names of rooms in the hotel correspond to frequencies and cities in which the station broadcasts.

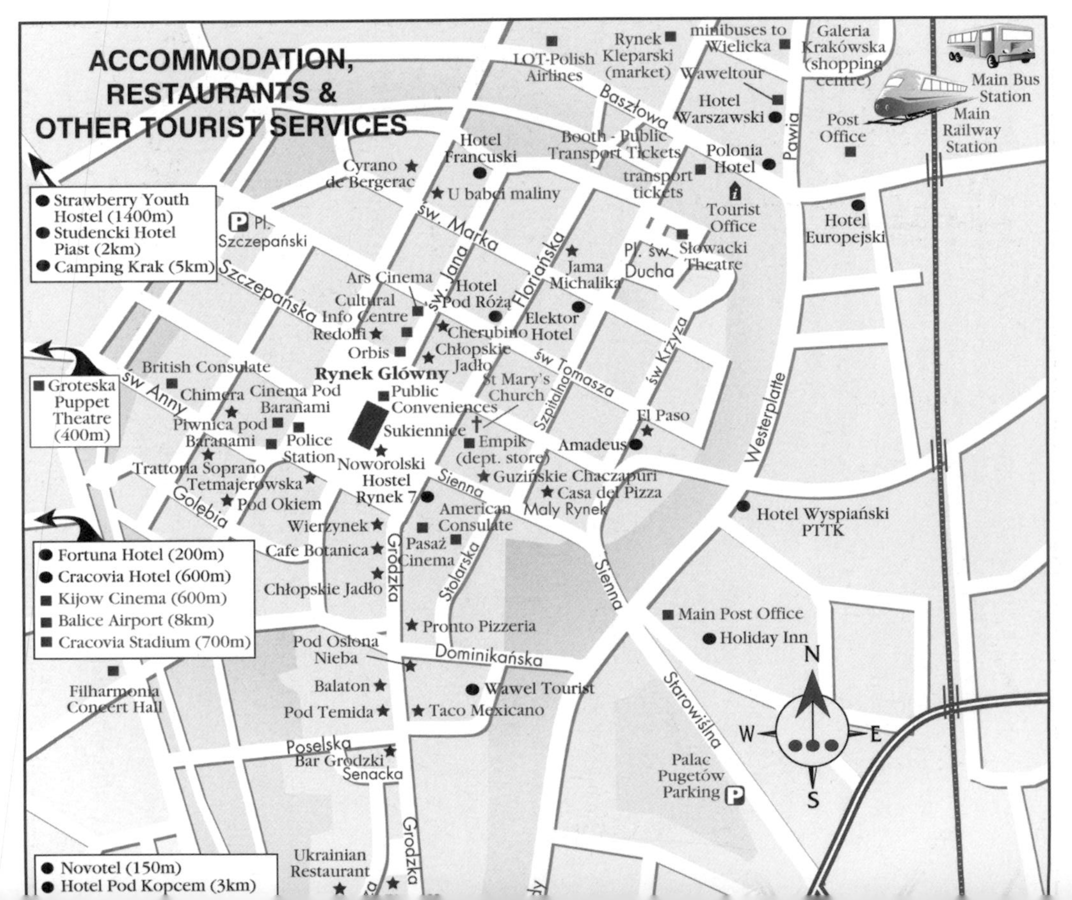

ACCOMMODATION, RESTAURANTS & OTHER TOURIST SERVICES
Strawberry Youth Hostel (1400m)
Studencki Hotel Piast (2km)
Camping Krak (5km)
Groteska Puppet Theatre (400m)
Fortuna Hotel (200m)
Cracovia Hotel (600m)
Kijow Cinema (600m)
Balice Airport (8km)
Cracovia Stadium (700m)
Novotel (150m)
Hotel Pod Kopcem (3km)
LOT-Polish Airlines
Rynek Kleparski (market)
minibuses to Wielicka
Galeria Krakówska (shopping centre)
Main Bus Station
Main Railway Station
Waweltour
Hotel Warszawski
Post Office
Baszłowa
Pawia
Booth - Public Transport Tickets
transport tickets
Polonia Hotel
Tourist Office
Hotel Europejski
Hotel Francuski
Cyrano de Bergerac
U babci maliny
św. Marka
Pl. Szczepański
Szczepańska
Floriańska
Jama Michalika
Pl. św. Ducha
Słowacki Theatre
Ars Cinema
św. Jana
Hotel Pod Różą
Cultural Info Centre
Elektor Hotel
Cherubino
Redolfi
Chłopskie Jadło
Orbis
św Tomasza
św Krzyża
British Consulate
Rynek Główny
St Mary's Church
św Anny
Chimera
Cinema Pod Baranami
Public Conveniences
Szpitalna
El Paso
Westerplatte
Piwnica pod Baranami
Police Station
Sukiennice
Empik (dept. store)
Amadeus
Trattoria Soprano
Noworolski
Tetmajerowska
Hostel Rynek 7
Sienna
Guzińskie Chaczapuri
Casa del Pizza
Pod Okiem
Gołębia
American Consulate
Mały Rynek
Hotel Wyspiański PTTK
Wierzynek
Cafe Botanica
Grodzka
Pasaż Cinema
Stolarska
Chłopskie Jadło
Pronto Pizzeria
Main Post Office
Holiday Inn
Pod Osłoną Nieba
Dominikańska
Filharmonia Concert Hall
Balaton
Wawel Tourist
Starowiślna
Pod Temida
Taco Mexicano
N
W
E
S
Poselska
Bar Grodzki
Senacka
Palac Pugetów Parking
Ukrainian Restaurant

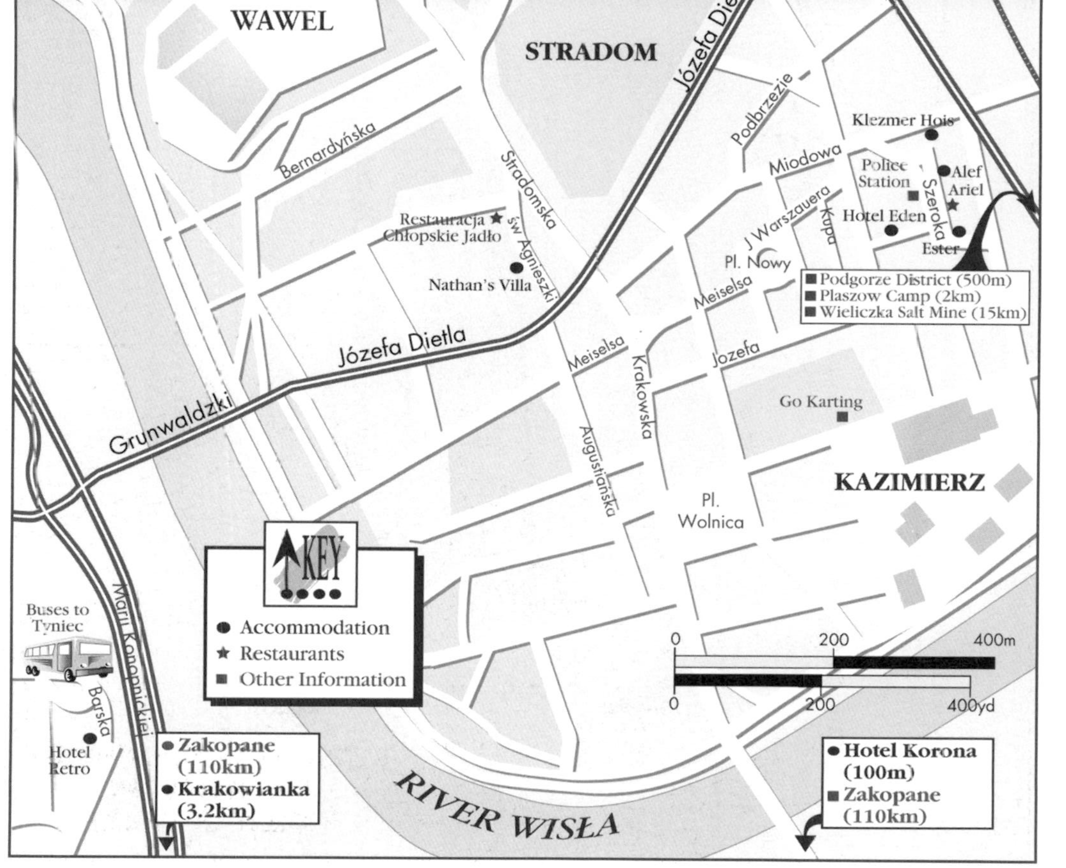
WAWEL
STRADOM
KAZIMIERZ
RIVER WISŁA
Józefa Dietla
Grunwaldzki
Bernardyńska
Stradomska
św Agnieszki
Restauracja Chłopskie Jadło
Nathan's Villa
Meiselsa
Augustiańska
Krakowska
Józefa
Pl. Wolnica
Go Karting
Pl. Nowy
J Warszauera
Kupa
Miodowa
Podbrzezie
Klezmer Hois
Police Station
Hotel Eden
Szeroka
Alef
Ariel
Ester
Podgorze District (500m)
Plaszow Camp (2km)
Wieliczka Salt Mine (15km)
KEY
Accommodation
Restaurants
Other Information
0
200
400m
0
200
400yd
Hotel Korona (100m)
Zakopane (110km)
Zakopane (110km)
Krakowianka (3.2km)
Marii Konopnickiej
Barska
Hotel Retro
Buses to Tyniec

Amadeus $$$$

Mikołajska 20
☎ (012) 429 6070
fax (012) 429 6062
www.hotel-amadeus.pl
email: amadeus@janpol.com.pl
Excellent small hotel occupying a recently-renovated mansion situated very close to the Rynek Główny. Reasonably plush rooms and high standard of service.

Hotel Copernicus $$$$

Kanonicza 16
☎ (012) 424 3400
fax (012) 424 3405
copernicus@hotel.com.pl
Ultra-smart hotel situated in a Gothic building on a very quiet street between the castle and the main square. Huge, high-ceilinged rooms, and a sense of refined opulence throughout. Rather more personal than bigger hotels in this price bracket, and recommended for those who can afford it.

Holiday Inn $$$$

Wielopole 4
☎ (012) 6190000 (UK) 0800 897121
fax (012) 619 0005
www.holidayinn.com
New hotel located very close to the main square and aimed at business travellers: regular Holiday Inn customers know what they're in for. A big hotel with a confident bland shininess about it which cannot hide its rather soulless flavour, although rooms are undeniably comfortable. Rates are cheaper at weekends and during the winter and it's worth enquiring about any offers.

Cracovia Hotel $$$$

al. Focha 1
☎ (012) 424 5670
fax (012) 424 5632
email: rez.cracovia@orbis.pl
Huge, spacious hotel located 10 minute walk west of the centre of town. Still owned and operated by Orbis, the state-owned travel and tourist company. Characterless but very comfortable; betrays its functional 1960s origins despite numerous renovations. The *Błonia* open fields, once a cavalry training ground for the army and more recently the venue for open-air Papal masses, are situated across the road. Websites such as Expedia (see p.126) often have some very good price deals for this hotel – especially during the winter.

Elektor Hotel $$$$

ul. Szpitalna 28
☎ (012) 423 2317
fax (012) 423 2327
email: elektor@bci.Kraków.pl
www.hotelelektor.com.pl
Small, pricey hotel located in a quiet street near the centre of town, half-way between the station and the main square; smart and refined, with well-appointed rooms. An expensive hotel which doesn't fall into the trap of being bland and soulless as do others in this price category. VIPs often stay here; guests have included the Crown Prince of Japan – while the Queen of England has dined in the restaurant (see p.146).

Novotel Kraków Centrum $$$$

Tadeusza Kościuszki 5
☎ (012) 299 2900
fax (012) 299 2999
email: H3372@accor.com
www.novotel.com
This new four star hotel is located on the north bank of the River Wisła, 1km southwest of the Rynek Główny and 600m west of Wawel. Part of the Accor and Novotel hotel chains it has large, comfortable rooms, a health club, a swimming pool and even a 'kids corner' with Sony Playstations to keep younger guests amused. Like many hotels in this category, however, it could be anywhere, and its location in a fairly ordinary part of town is rather uninspiring.

Car Hire

Joka Rent a Car

Starowiślna 13
☎ (012) 429 6630

Avis

Ul. Lubicz 23 ☎ (012) 629 6108

rentacar

Ul Piłsudskiego 19
☎ (012) 618 4330; fax (012) 618 4330
Website: www.e-rentacar.pl

Hertz

Airport: ☎ (012) 637 1120
City: al. Focha 1
☎ (012) 637 1120
fax (012) 422 2930
International booking number from UK: ☎ 08705 996699
email: hertz_hq@pol.pl
website: www.hertz.com

Children

Kraków's tourism tends to rely on a heavy diet of museums, churches, palaces and high culture. However there are some alternative activities that are definitively more child-friendly. These would include a sight-seeing trip around the town centre by horse-drawn carriage (tours start from the Rynek Główny), a visit to the Wieliczka Salt Mine (p.000), or to the Dragon's Den in the Wawel (p.000). There are opera and classical music concerts for children on Saturday mornings (check out the programme of events for the Filharmonia and other venues listed in the following section). Children will also enjoy the puppet theatre and the zoo. Teenagers might appreciate a visit to Auschwitz-Birkenau, bearing in mind how prominently the Holocaust features on UK History syllabuses. In terms of allowing children to let off steam, there is a go-karting track *(Motodrom Gokartowy)* housed in an old tram shed at ul.sw.Wawrzyńca 12 in Kazimierz (open daily noon-11pm; children aged 7+ only); and a water park, the *Park Wodny,* situated in the northern suburbs and featuring water slides, climbing walls, a 'wild river', and various pools (all with lifeguards present), and Jacuzzis and saunas for parents, at ul.Dobrego Pasterza 126 (☎ 012 616 3190; www.ParkWodny.pl). Children might also like the opportunities for bowling, tennis-playing, outdoor swimming or horse riding in the city; a rafting trip on the River Dunajec is the most appropriate excursion beyond the city for children; while a visit to a football match might also be welcome – however these are heavily policed because of hooligans and the atmosphere might seem rather intimidating.

The Topolina Agency (☎ 012 633 0662/0501 617338) at Jozefa Friedleina 31 offers a babysitting service. Babysitters speak English.

Culture and Entertainment

In recent years Kraków has developed into a cultural centre of world importance, and to acknowledge this fact the European Union Ministers of Culture designated the city one of the nine 'European Cities of Culture' for the year 2000. A year of cultural events was overseen by the patronage of the city's leading cultural residents, the film director Andrzej Wajda and the composer Krzysztof Penderecki. The Kraków 2000 Festival stretched from 1996 to 2000 and embraced art, theatre, literature and music; since the millennium year the city has continued to trade on the "Kraków 2000" image, which is still used in advertising and other promotional literature for the city.

Information about the current cultural scene in the city is best obtained from the **Cultural Information Centre** *(Centrum Informacji Kulturalnej)* on ul. św. Jana 2, just off the Rynek Główny (open Mon-Sat 10am-6pm; ☎ 421 7787). Here you can buy tickets for some events, pick up leaflets and flyers, and buy the *Karnet: Kraków Cultural Events* booklet, which is published every month. This is essentially an invaluable listings guide, published in Polish and English, with daily **information** on dance performances, concerts, exhibitions, opera, theatre, jazz and film. The booklet is also available at tourist offices and in hotels, and its contents are also available online at www.karnet.Kraków.pl. Other English-language publications include *Kraków in your Pocket*, a listings guide in English published every two months and available from bookshops and news stands, and *City Magazine*, which tends to concentrate more on the trendy bar and club scene.

Cinemas tend to show films in their original language with Polish subtitles. European art house films as well as the latest American blockbusters are popular. One of the best cinemas in town is the *Cinema Pod Baranami*, situated in the south-west corner of Rynek Główny and showing an eclectic mix of recent and not-so-recent European and American films. The *Pasaż* at Rynek Główny 9 is also worth a look if you are interested in seeing off-beat films, as is the five-screen *Ars* cinema at św.Jana 6, just north of the Rynek Główny. For big-screen Hollywood blockbuster action there are some multiplex cinemas in the suburbs, all of which go under the banner of *Cinema City*; the biggest cinema in the centre of town is the *Kijow*, situated immediately behind the Cracovia hotel at Krasinskiego 34. Film festivals are included in the list of annual cultural events, while day-today film listings are given in the *Karnet*.

Jazz has a constant presence in Kraków, which sees itself as lying at the heart of the Polish jazz scene. Check out venues listed in the *Karnet*, or head for the main jazz cellars in town such as the *Harris Piano Jazz Bar* at Rynek Główny 28, *Kornet* at Krasinskiego 9, or *Jazz u.Muniaka* at the south end of Floriańska, where copious quantities of home-grown jazz and beer usually flow until the early hours in summer (in winter performances may only be on Thu, Fri and Sat). **Rock music** concerts are often advertised on flyposters and are listed in the "Music" section of the *Karnet*; concerts include touring foreign bands in addition to gigs staged by home-grown Polish groups.

Poland has a proud tradition of **classical music**. Its most famous composer is Frederick Chopin, who was influenced by the folk music of Masovia, his native region; in the 1990s Henryk Gorecki was prominent in the classical CD bestseller lists. Musical ensembles such as the Kraków and Warsaw Philharmonic Orchestras are renowned the world over, and much of their repertoire features music by the country's national composers. The premier **venue** for classical music concerts is the Filharmonia, to the south-west of the Rynek Główny at the corner of Podwale and Straszewskiego. The venue is home to the Kraków Philharmonic Orchestra and the Capella Cracoviensis (the city's best-known choir); it also plays hosts to many visiting international artists and groups (www.filharmonia.Kraków.pl; box office open Mon-Fri noon-7pm and one hour before performances on Saturdays; ☎ 012 429 1345/012 422 9477). There are many other concert venues in the city, including the Kraków Music Academy on ul.św. Tomasza 43; some concerts take place in the open air in summer. Chamber and organ recitals take place in the Krzysztofory Palace, the Collegium Maius, and in churches, particularly St Mary's on the main square. Tyniec Abbey to the west of the city is also famous for its organ recitals. The Słowacki Theatre is the main venue for **opera and ballet** and is home to the Kraków Opera; the Scena Opretkowa, home to the Kraków Operetta, is at ul.Lubicz 48. If you want to see an opera in Kraków be warned that seats sell out a long time in advance-book from home, if possible. All music and opera performances are listed in the *Karnet*. There is no permanent ballet company and most dance performances are associated with the Spring Ballet Festival and the International Ballet Festival.

Although there are obvious language difficulties, those who are interested in the **theatre** might find a visit to a play worthwhile. The *Karnet* has listings of productions but only in the Polish-language section of the magazine; understandably, plays performed in Polish are rarely listed or reviewed in English-language tourist-oriented publications. (The British Council, whose offices are on the east side of the Rynek Główny, will be able to provide any details of visiting theatre companies performing in English.) Back in the 1960s the director Tadeusz Kantor placed Kraków firmly on the contemporary theatre scene with his groundbreaking productions at the Cricot 2 Theatre (which is no longer active, although mementoes of plays staged here can be seen in the Theatre Museum). Nowadays the theatrical tradition in the city remains varied and strong. The Słowacki Theatre (see immediately above) stages classic Polish plays, and smaller-scale productions can be seen at other venues including the Bagatela on Karmelicka and the Stary Theatre at Jagiellońska 1 – where you will sometimes find the plays of Shakespeare and other world dramatists staged in Polish. The Teatr Lalki I Maski Groteska, at Skarbowa 2, is a **puppet theatre**, with shows for children staged in the day and more satirically-minded shows for adults staged in the evening. Shows incorporate live actors as well as puppets and incorporate stories from Homer to traditional fairy tales.

A staple of Kraków entertainment is the **cabaret**, incorporating musical, comedy, and satirical numbers; the late-evening events are hugely popular with Cracovians, and visitors can latch onto parts of the performance, even if they don't speak any Polish. One of the most famous cabarets takes place in the dark, intimate surroundings of the Pod Baranami bar/jazz cellar, located where św.Anny meets the Rynek Główny. Tickets can be obtained from the third floor of the Malopolska Cultural Centre at 25 Rynek Główny, across from the pod Baranami (head for the door marked "Administraja"; open 11am-5pm weekdays). Details of other cabarets can be found in the *karnet*.

In terms of **clubs**, check out the *Karnet* or head for the Roentgen at pl.Szczepański 3 (trance, house, acid jazz); Strefa 22 at Rynek Główny 22 (drum'n'bass, techno and acid jazz); Wolnosc FM at Krolewska 1 (one of the largest clubs, specializing in house, dance and soul music); Kredens at Rynek Główny 12 and Jazz Rock Café at Sławkowska 12 (both disco-pubs); the Pub Studencki DNS at Budryka 6 (known as the 'Swiniarnia' – a student club and beer hall featuring billiards and darts); or the Rotunda at Oleandry 1 (another large student club that stages live rock or jazz events).

Cultural and Religious Festivals

January 6 (Ephiphany)

Carol singers move from house to house, and chalk the letters K, M and B on doorways. The letters stand for Kaspar, Melchior and Balthasar, who were the Three Kings.

Mid January

Festival of Orthodox Church Music.

February 2

Feast of St Mary Gromniczna. Wax candles lit in churches.

Late February

Four-day festivals of sea shanties

March

International **Festival of Alternative Theatre**, and international **Jazz Festival** for Young Musicians, both at the Rotunda Club.

March 23

Topienie Marzanny – a festival symbolizing the end of winter. Children throw small dolls, representing winter, into rivers.

Last Thursday before Lent

Tłusty czwartek. Doughnuts are eaten on a feast day whose name translates as "Fat Thursday".

Palm Sunday (Niedziela Palmowa)

Decorated palms are paraded into churches. There is a famous and long-standing competition for the best-decorated palm at Lipnica Murawana, a village 40km east of Kraków. Poland's most famous Palm Sunday procession takes place in Kalwaria Zebrzydowska, 30km southwest of Krakow, where Passion Plays are performed on Maundy Thursday and Good Friday in a tradition dating back to the seventeenth century; the events of the Crucifixion are re-enacted in the shadow of a Baroque monastery.

Holy Saturday

Easter food is taken to churches and blessed.

Easter Sunday

Most important religious festival of the year. Masses said in churches throughout the day.

Easter Monday

Emmaus Fair in Zwierzyniec, in the west of the city and along Kościuszko Street. On this day there is a tradition whereby girls are doused with water by boys, which has its roots in ancient fertility rituals; however these days it would appear everyone gets a soaking.

Pentecost

Bonfires lit on hilltops in the region around Kraków.

April

International Festival of Organ Music. A 40-year-old tradition which takes place over one week; **Cabaret festival** attracting satirists from all over the world.

April/May

Student Song Festival - open-air free concerts on the main square, in a festival dating from the 1960s.

May 3

Constitution Day. Most important secular holiday in Poland, marking the adoption of the first Polish constitution in 1791.

First Sunday after May 8

Procession from Wawel to Pauline Church on the Rock where the relics of the Patron Saints of Poland are carried through the streets to mark the **Feast of St Stanisław**.

May

Ballet festival, with a mix of classical and modern performances in the Słowacki Theatre; **Juvenalia**, a student carnival, when keys to the town gates are handed over in a ceremony featuring parades and music; and the **Kraków Film Festival**, held at the end of the month, which concentrates on short documentary and fiction films (the main venue is the Kijow cinema; (www.cracowfilmfestival.pl)

May-September in even years (2008, 2010 etc)

Graphic Art Festival

May/June

Enthronement of the Rifle Club Champion. A procession and competition, with participants dressed in national costumes. The Marksmen's Brotherhood is a guild of crafsmen whose leader is the winner of an annual competition in which a silver cockerel is shot. The Champion Rifle Shot is enthroned in the Rynek Główny in a special ceremony.

Corpus Christi (Boże Ciało)

Religious Processions in churches. Main procession in Kraków takes place from Wawel to Rynek Główny.

May/June

(Thursday after Corpus Christi): **Lajkonik procession** from the convent in Zwierzyniec to the Rynek Główny. This features musicians and a magnificently-decorated hobby horse (the Lajkonik) which has peacock feathers attached to its head, and which is ridden through the streets of the city. Streets followed include Kościuszki, Zwierzyniecka and Grodzka which brings the procession to the Rynek, where the City Mayor presents the Lajkonik with a symbolic goblet of wine and a ransom. There are dances, fireworks and music. The procession takes anything up to six hours. During it the leader of the procession, the Khan, may strike passers-by with a mace to bring them good luck. The event commemorates the defeat of a Tartar invasion in the Middle Ages by a local clansman and is around two centuries old. Some of the original costumes, including the Khan's costume from 1904 designed by Stanisław Wyspiański, can be seen in the History Museum.

23rd, 24th June

Floating of the Wreaths. Amateur and professional folklore groups perform on a stage erected close to the Castle, floating illuminated wreaths on the river. The festival is held on St John the Baptist's and St Wanda's Days and is a commemoration of Midsummer's day. There are also boat parades and fireworks.

June

Festival of **Military Bands.**

June/July

Festival of Jewish Culture, including theatre, film, music and art. The event ends with an open-air concert on Szeroka, at the heart of Jewish Kraków, at the beginning of July; Organ recitals in Tyniec Abbey (see p.100) and St Mary's Church, mostly on Sundays.

July

Opera, International Street Theatre (mainly in the Rynek Główny), **Early Music** (with concerts mainly in churches) and International **Clarinet festivals**.

July

The **Wawel Jazz festival** in late July, a festival dating from 1999, features concerts in the open-air courtyards in Wawel.

August

Classical Music (last two weeks). Performances in concert halls, churches and other venues, with top international performers attracted to this very prestigious festival. **Highland folklore festival** in Zakopane (p.000) with some events in Kraków too, attracting folklore groups from all over the world.

August 15

Assumption of the Virgin Mary. Solemn masses in churches and major pilgrimage day in Częstochowa.

September

International Modern Chamber Music Competition and **Festival of Jazz Trumpeters.** Festival of **Folk Art** in Rynek Główny.

October 1 (approx)

Start of academic year at the Jagiellonian University. Academics and university officials parade through town in gowns.

October

Festival of Early Music (music from Baroque and Renaissance times performed on period instruments); **Jazz music festival; festival of forgotten music** (dedicated to traditional Slavic folk music).

November 1

All Saints Day. A day of national remembrance, when wreaths and candles are laid on tombstones and cemeteries are crowded with families remembering their dead. Turkish honey (sweets consisting of caramelized sugar with pistachios and walnuts) is on sale at cemetery gates.

November 11

Independence Day. Mass is said at Wawel Cathedral and a wreath is laid on the Tomb of the Unknown Soldier in pl.Jana Matejko, immediately north of the Barbican.

November

Festival of Animated Films (beginning of month).

December

International Ballet Festival (mid-month), and the **Silent Film Festival**. The latter is one of the few silent film festival in the world, with films shown to the accompaniment of pianists or jazz bands.

Christmas

Szopki – the exhibition of **traditional nativity cribs**. A meat-free meal is traditionally eaten on Christmas Eve and Midnight Masses are said after the ringing of the Zygmunt Bell at Wawel.

New Year

Huge crowds throng the Rynek Główny to see in the New Year.

Currency: Banks, Credit Cards & Costs

The **currency** in Poland is the *złoty*, abbreviated (in Poland and in this book) to zł (and occasionally to NPL, which stands for "New Polish Złotys" and refers to the currency reforms of 1995 when the złoty was re-valued). There are notes for 10, 20, 50, 100 and 200zł, with coins for 1, 2 5 and 10 zł. The złoty is divided into 100 *groszy*, for which there are coins valued at 50, 20, 10 and 5. At the time of writing the exchange rate was around 6zł to the pound sterling and 3.40 to the US dollar. Prices for services used by tourists are often quoted in euros, although payment is rarely, if ever, accepted in this currency.

There are **automatic cash machines** all over the centre of Kraków, especially around the Rynek Główny and along Floriańska, and at the railway station and airport. If you have credit or debit cards with Visa or Mastercard symbols, you can use them to withdraw złotys at any of these machines, which are easy to use (you can opt for instructions in English). However the machines break down more often than they might do back home and it is always useful to have a back-up supply of banknotes or travellers' cheques for these occasions.

Don't change **travellers' cheques** at banks (open 7.30am-5pm weekdays, and until 2pm on Saturdays) – there are lots in the centre of Kraków, but you will age visibly in the time it takes for all the form-filling to be done; the fastest place to change money and cheques is at the exchange counter in the main Orbis office on Rynek Główny (open 9am-6pm weekdays and until 2pm on Saturdays).

All over the centre of town are *kantor* offices, which are **private exchange centres**; they usually only take cash, but they are open long hours and at weekends, which means you might have to resort to using them when other places are closed. It is worth shopping around for the best rates as they vary considerably between kantor offices.

Polish money can be obtained from most UK banks on order. Credit and debit cards are used as widely in Kraków as they are in Western Europe.

In terms of **costs**, Kraków is still a reasonably inexpensive place to visit, although inflation and tourism have pushed prices up in recent years and Poland is no longer the ultra-cheap place to visit that it was in the recent past. You will find alcoholic drinks, food, restaurants and entrance fees very reasonable priced; public transport is extremely cheap but, in comparison, accommodation prices are fast approaching those of Western Europe.

Customs Regulations

On entering Poland you are allowed to carry, and do not have to declare, up to two still cameras, one video camera, 250 cigarettes or 50 cigars or 250g (8oz) of pipe tobacco, and medicines and electrical goods which are obviously for your own personal use. Import and export of unlimited amounts of foreign currency is allowed; there are no currency declaration forms.

On leaving Poland you are allowed to export gifts and souvenirs to a value of US$100 without paying duty. If you purchase a work of art, get some sort of written evidence of its age, as the export of books, paintings and sculptures produced in Poland or elsewhere before 1945 is illegal without a special permit (see p.149).

Diplomatic Representation

Polish Embassy in London

47 Portland Place, London W1N 4JH, ☎ 020 7580 4324.

Polish Consulate in London

73 New Cavendish Street, London W1N 8HQ, ☎ 020 7580 0476.

Polish Embassy in Washington

2640 16th St NW, Washington DC 20009 ☎ 202 234 3800

Other Polish consultes in the USA

Chicago ☎ 312 337 8166; New York ☎ 212 561 8160; Los Angeles ☎ 310 442 8500.

British Embassy in Warsaw

Al Róż 1, ☎ (022) 311 0000.

American Embassy in Warsaw

al.Ujazdowskie 29, ☎ 022 504 2000

American Consulate in Kraków

ul. Stolarska 9, ☎ (012) 424 5100

Honorary Consulate of the UK in Kraków

ul św Anny 9 ☎(012) 421 7030

Driving Information

In terms of **rules and regulations**, you should rive on the right; safety belts are compulsory and must be used on any car fitted with them; driving under the influence of *any* amount of alcohol is illegal; speed limits are 60kph (37mph) within city limits, 90kph (56mph) outside city limits, 110 kph (68mph) on designated fast roads, and 130 kph (81mph) on motorways; speaking on a mobile phone while driving is illegal (unless it's a hands-free set); cars must be equipped by law with a warning triangle and a fire extinguisher; children under 12 cannot travel in the front seats and any child under 150cm/4 ft 11inches in height must travel in a child seat; carry a drivers' licence from your home country; and headlights must be switched on at all times when driving between November and March.

In terms of potential **hazards and problems**, drivers in Kraków have to cope with narrow streets, a one-way system, trams (which always have right of way – never overtake them when they are stopped), traffic congestion and parking restrictions which are maintained throughout the city centre. Illegally-parked cars are towed away. Much of the city centre is pedestrianized and with most places within walking distance or a short tram-ride, driving in the city is not advised. Always **park** in guarded car-parks in towns *(parking strzezony)* as thefts from parked cars are reasonably common. Parking areas are marked on the map on p.122-123 and include Plac Szczepanski and the car park behind the Pałac Pugetów on Starowiślna, southeast of the Rynek Główny. The roof above the main railway station platforms forms a large car parking area but is slightly further away from the city centre. Illegally-parked cars are clamped. The telephone number you should use to get yourself unclamped will be printed on the back of the penalty notice on the windscreen.

Be aware that the central part of the city is divided into **zones** as far as drivers are concerned. No vehicles can enter zone A (the area around the Rynek Główny); zone B (which extends to the Planty) requires a permit to enter which foreigners are unlikely to be able to get hold of (although you can drive to your hotel in zone B if it has a car park); and zone C, where you can drive, but where parking is very restricted (and requires a permit). Zones are marked on signposts (*Strefa A, Strefa B* etc).

Beyond the city, watch out for mopeds and slow-moving horse and cart traffic. The national breakdown number is ☎ 9637. *Benzyna* (**petrol**) is available in 94 and 95 octane leaded and 94,95 and 98 octane unleaded. Diesel fuel is known as diesel or *olej napędowy*. There are plenty of filling stations on roads leading out of Kraków, including those operated by some internationally-recognized names such as BP.

Electricity

Voltage in Poland is the standard European 220 volts, 50 cycle AC. Twin-point sockets are used everywhere, and you'll need a continental adaptor if you want to use electrical devices brought from the UK.

Health

EU citizens are entitled to free emergency health care in Poland provided they have a stamped and completed E111 form. You will probably have to pay for medicines. Non-EU citizens should take out comprehensive medical insurance before coming to Poland, and this is highly advisable for EU citizens too, as lengthy courses of treatment must be paid for even by holders of E111 forms.

Basic complaints can be dealt with by pharmacies (*apteka*), where a little English will probably be spoken; try those at Grodzka 26 or Rynek Główny 13. There is always at least one pharmacy open 24 hours; hotels should know which one, or look in local newspapers or tourist guides. (The pharmacy attached to the Tesco hypermarket in the southern suburbs is open 24 hours but is rather awkward to reach from the town centre, see p.148) If you need to see a doctor, it's best to get your hotel to contact one, although the US or UK consulates might provide some English-speaking help and advice (see p.135). Treatment in a private hospital will be better and of course more expensive than in state hospitals *(szpital)*; Medicover at ul. Raklowicka 7 (☎ 012 616 1000; www.medicover.com.pl) is a private clinic offering the services of English-speaking doctors and dentists.

An Ambulance can be summoned by dialling ☎ 999.

Tap water is safe to drink but most prefer to drink bottled water, which is widely available. Contraceptives *(prezerwatywy* is polish for condoms) can be hard to obtain (not surprisingly in one of the most fervently Catholic cities in the world), but most other sorts of medicine can be obtained over the counter in *apteka* (*podpaski*are sanitary towels, *tampony* are tompons).

Internet cafés

Internet cafés have sprung up all over the city and are very cheap to use; one to try in the centre is Pl@net, on the southwest side of the Rynek Główny, diagonally across from the south end of the Sukiennice, which is open 24 hours; there are plenty of others, particularly along Floriańska.

Maps

The best city map is the *Copernicus Plan Miasta: Kraków* produced by PPWK (Warsaw). It's easy to buy in the city (try *Empik* on the east side of the Rynek Główny, or news stands at the station), and includes a street index and an enlarged plan of the central area. It's aimed at residents as well as visitors, and worth getting, even if you're only here for a short while; you'll need it to identify features not in the centre of town such as the Kościuszko Mound (with its restaurant and hotel), the Cracovia Hotel, the Youth Hostels, and Płaszów station, none of which are shown on the maps in this book. In addition the map includes many of the places described in chapter four, and all the tram and bus routes in the city centre and outskirts.

Measurements

Metric measurements operate in Poland. Eight kilometres equals five miles, 1kg weighs just over 2lb, and 1 litre is just under 2 pints.

Media and Books

Surprisingly, for a city with so many English-speaking visitors, it can be hard getting hold of British and American **newspapers** here. The stall just off the booking hall of the main railway station is the place to buy copies of the *International Guardian*, the *International Herald Tribune* and most UK papers such as the *Times* and *Telegraph*; they tend to run out of stock by the afternoon, though. Some of the more expensive hotels, such as the Cracovia or the Novotel, also stock newspapers. The *Empic* department store on the south-east side of the Rynek Główny normally stocks a good selection of foreign newspapers and magazines just inside the front door.

The BBC World Service can be picked up in the city on 12095, 9410, 6195 and 5875 MHZ. Local independent **radio** stations have news bulletins in English, and state radio sometimes broadcasts BBC radio programmes in English; twiddle the dial and you might get a surprise. The most expensive hotels have cable/satellite **TV** carrying MTV, CNN. Deutsche Welle (German international TV which is often broadcast in English) and BBC World television. Polish television stations tend to offer a diet of gameshows and soaps, with bought-in programming from the USA, UK or Germany dubbed by a single *lektor* who reads all the parts in the same voice.

Opening Times

Opening times for specific museums and other attractions are given in the text; most close on a Monday, with free entrance on one of the days (often Sunday or Saturday). Opening hours are curtailed between November and March. City-centre churches are generally kept open all the time, although they will close to tourists during concerts and services (which are frequent). Kraków is a tourist-oriented city and most shops keep long hours, some even opening on Sundays, although most are open 10am-6pm weekdays and 10am-3pm Saturdays (the Tesco hypermarket in the southern suburbs is open 24 hours – see p.148); bars and clubs are open long into the early hours, although some may shut on Monday.

Passports

Citizens of the UK, Ireland, Canada, Australia, New Zealand and the USA need only their passport to enter Poland; they can then stay for a period of up to 90 days (180 days for UK and Ireland). Other nationalities may require visas and should consult Polish consulates in this regard (see p.134-135). Passports are usually examined closely; they must be valid for six months beyond the last day of your stay in Poland. You must keep your passport with you at all times in Poland, even though the chances of you being stopped and asked for it are slim.

Police and security

Theft is unfortunately a growing problem in Poland and thieves often target foreigners; in particular, beware of pickpockets in busy areas such as railway stations, markets, and on trams and buses, where they will often operate in groups to create a distraction by a sudden shove or push. Take special care if you are driving, as theft from parked cars is comparatively common. If you are the victim of a theft you will need to report it to the police; the main police station in the centre of town is at Szeroka 35 in Kazimierz but there is a small police station on the western side of the Rynek Główny, near the junction with sw.Anny.

Post

Post offices are signified by the word *Poczta*. There are two in the centre of Kraków – the main post office (*Poczta Główna)*, which is on the corner of Wielopole and Westerplatte, 300m (300 yards) east of the main square; and a second office close to the station (see map, pp.130-131). The second office is actually easier to use and in theory is open 24 hours a day; the main post office is open 7.30am-8.30pm Mon-Fri, 8am-2pm Sat and 9-11am Sun.

Some hotels sell basic things like stamps for postcards. Make sure *anything* you send goes air mail (*lotnicza*) otherwise it will go surface, taking six weeks to reach the UK rather than about 4 days. You can obtain *lotnicza* stickers from post offices.

Local letters should be posted in green post boxes; all other letters should go in the red boxes.

DHL has an office at Ul. Zawila 61.

Public Conveniences

Most public conveniences *(toalety* or *ubikacja*) are reasonably clean, and kept so by a ferocious guardian who will demand 1zł from you for using the facilities. This even includes a few restaurants – even if you are dining in them. There are public conveniences at the north and south end of the Sukiennice in the main square. The gents (*męskie*) is often marked by a triangle pointing downwards; ladies *(damskie)* by a circle or a triangle pointing upwards.

Public Holidays

National Public Holidays include:

January 1	(New Year)
Easter Monday	
May 1	(Labour Day)
May 3	(Constitution Day)
May/June	(Corpus Christi)
August 15	(Feast of the Assumption)
November 1	(All Saints Day)
November 11	(National Independence Day)
December 25/26	(Christmas)

Public transport will normally be reduced on these days and most shops, and some attractions such as museums, will also be closed; on religious festival days, of course, churches are even busier than usual.

Religious services

There is a Catholic church service in English every Sunday at 10.30am at St Giles' Church, Grodszka 57. There is no mosque in Kraków. However there is a Muslim prayer meeting held in the lecture room of the department of Polish Language at the Technical University, Skarżyńskiego 1, every Friday between noon and 2pm.

Restaurants

The centre of Kraków boasts dozens of eateries, from smart and elegant restaurants serving traditional Polish food to familiar Western high-street restaurant chains. A number of ethnic restaurants have also appeared on the scene. Prices are generally cheap for Western visitors.

Like many cities in the old Eastern Europe, Kraków gets up earlier and goes to bed earlier than you might be used to, and many restaurants close at 10pm or earlier. If you plan to eat around 8pm, it is wise to book in advance; more than an hour or so either side of 8pm, you should have no problem getting a table if you just turn up.

Most restaurants close by midnight; those that are open 24 hours include the restaurant at the station, which is quite acceptable. **Street food**, sold around the Rynek Główny and streets such as Floriańska and Grodzka, includes bagels or pretzels, coated with salt crystals or poppy or sesame seeds; boiled corn-on-the-cob; grilled sausages; and in the autumn, roasted chestnuts.

Inexpensive

Casa del Pizza

Maly Rynek

Wide ranges of pizzas and pasta dishes; plus fish, grills, soups, salads and desserts. An ideal place for lunch, on a square adjacent to the Rynek Główny but which sees far less passing tourist traffic.

El Paso

św. Krzyża

Tex-Mex restaurant situated in a quiet side street just east of the Rynek Główny. Plenty of pork, beef and chicken dishes with a few vegetarian dishes on offer; possibilities include meat and bean taco with fajitas. A limited selection of Russian and traditional Polish food is available too.

McDonald's

Floriańska 55

The chain's main and original outlet in the centre of town (others have appeared in recent years, in both the town centre and outskirts) occupies prime position between the station and the Rynek Główny, right on the main shopping street. It serves up just what you'd expect, daily from 7am to 2am. Part of the downstairs area is located in some interestingly cavernous cellars, while there is a pleasant outdoor area available in summer.

Pronto Pizzeria

corner of Dominikanska and
Grodzka (north side).
Filling and moderately-priced pizzas; cold starters and various meat or vegetarian dishes on offer in a partly self-service restaurant. Shish kebab and falafel dishes are on offer too. Nothing special, but you can eat outside in summer, watching the trams go by.

Pod Temidą and other 'milk bars'

Grodzka 43
This eatery on Grodzka, the road linking the Rynek Główny with Wawel, is a *bar mleczny* or 'milk bar', a uniquely Polish institution also known as *jadłodajnia* in Kraków. These cheap restaurants were hugely popular in Communist days but they're now something of a dying breed, particularly in the centre of Polish cities. This one serves big portions of fuctional, home-cooked food, such as stewed cabbage with meat and spices *(bigos)*, dumplings stuffed with meat, mushrooms, cottage cheese or onion *(pierogi)*, and potato pancakes in sour cream or goulash *(placki ziemniaczane).* Milk bars like Pod Temidą appeal to students, impecunious artists as well as passing tourists looking for a cheap and genuinely Polish place for lunch. The 'vegetarian' dishes contain no meat pieces but might be prepared with meat stock or lard made from animal fats. Other milk bars include *Bar Grodzki*, just a few doors away at Grodzka 47, and *U babci maliny* on Sławkowska, which is decked out like a typical Polish peasant's hut.

Trattoria Soprano

Corner of sw Anny and Jagiellońska
Convivial Italian restaurant in university quarter that is popular with Poles as well as tourists. The usual Italian fare on offer in another restaurant that makes for a good lunch stop.

Moderate

Pod Oslona Nieba

Oriental food (Tunisian and Arab specialities) including couscous, falafel, shish kebab and various salads and chicken dishes.

Gruzińskie Chaczapuri

Sienna and św.Marka
This restaurant has two branches, both of which specialize in the cuisine of the former Soviet republic of Georgia. The typically hearty meat, potato and vegetable dishes include cheese pie with chicken and various combinations of meat, rice, eggplant and vegetables, all covered in traditional spicy sauces; *chaczapuri* are bread cakes filled with cheese. Georgia has one of the most distinctive culinary traditions in central Asia and these restaurants are worth seeking out.

Ariel

Szeroka 18
Kosher restaurant in the Jewish Quarter, 20 minutes on foot from the Rynek Glówny but well worth seeking out. In summer tables are set out on the quiet, ancient square, while the homely interior of the restaurant is decorated with paintings depicting everything from boys being prepared for their Bar Mitzvah to traditional scenes from the Jewish Quarter. Beef, fish and poultry dishes (including goose) are on offer in poignant surroundings in a city where Jews once made up a third of the population, and where now the community numbers only a few hundred. In the evenings from 8.30pm onwards traditional Jewish folk music and songs are performed by a costumed group of musicians using instruments including a piano accordion, violins and clarinets. The music veers from joyful and rumbustious to the more melancholic and restrained, all of it celebrating and keeping alive a tradition

of music making which at one point looked doomed to extinction.

Alef

Szeroka 17

Adjacent to the *Ariel*, this restaurant also serves tasty traditional Jewish (but not strictly *kosher*) food, with live music in the evenings. Very attractive surroundings with a log fire burning in winter which, with the fact that this is also a hotel and there are two very friendly cats present, gives it a slightly homelier air to the *Ariel*. Dishes include gefilte fisch (stuffed carp), stuffed goose necks, and vine leaves filled with goose liver, almonds and raisins.

Balaton

Grodzka

Excellent and very popular Hungarian restaurant; everything's Hungarian – food, waiters, beer and menu. Beef, goulash and paprika dishes galore.

Chimera salad bar and restaurant

św. Anny 3

The salad bar in the Gothic cellars, popular with students, offers a buffet selection (including vegetarian dishes); choices on offer include baked potatoes and various asparagus dishes. There is a patio for outdoor dining in the summer. In the more high-brow restaurant, located on the ground floor, there is host of interesting dishes on offer, including hot beer soup with cheese, plum-stuffed sirloin croquettes, beetroot soup with cabbage, plenty of veal dishes, and seven different types of tea (and a glass of mead if you're here on a cold day in winter). Some dishes need to be ordered a day in advance, if you're that well organised. The restaurant is a venue for chamber concerts and small-scale drama productions.

Restauracja Chłopskie Jadło

św Agnieszki 1; other branches at Grodzka 9 and św.Jana 3

The original restaurant to open under the Chłopskie Jadło banner, at sw.Agnieszki 1, serves moderately-priced Polish food in a superbly "rustic" atmosphere (in fact it's so rustic some of the tables aren't even flat !). The place is decked out like a country inn in Poland, all wooden beams and benches, warmed by a roaring log fire in winter, with musicians dressed in folk costumes singing amidst the bundles of straw and hanging bunches of onions. The menu includes traditional pork and veal dishes, and offerings such as sauerkraut and duck, with lots of potatoes and vegetables – and all of it served in huge, hearty helpings. Located southeast of Wawel, on an otherwise unremarkable side street, this is a place well worth seeking out. In recent years the restaurant has opened two other branches, in Grodzka and ul.św.Jana, both of which are streets leading off the Rynek Główny. These serve similar food in similar surroundings but are rather less spacious than the original restaurant and, being much closer to the city centre, are also much more liable to be busy.

Pizza Hut

ul. Grodzka 57

Exactly the same as back home: open until 10pm daily. Cavernous ancient cellars downstairs have been well restored to make for an interesting dining area.

Ukrainian Restaurant

Kanonicza

Cool, intimate, cellar-bound restaurant close to the castle: on a warm day you'll retreat from the heat but not necessarily the crowds. Chicken and beef dishes, with big helpings, and heavy on potatoes and vegetables – plus a couple of Ukrainian specialities, just to justify the name.

Taco Mexicano

Poselska

Tex-Mex food featuring plenty of meats, beans and salad dishes, including chicken *fajitas* and pork chops in peanut sauce.

Cherubino

ul. św. Tomasza 15
This spacious restaurant, tucked away in a side street just north of the Rynek Główny, serves mainly Italian dishes, though with some Polish fare thrown in for good measure. The food itself is acceptable and the interior is attractive. Meat is prepared on grills placed in the centre of the dining area.

Expensive

Amadeus

Ul. Krzyża

A fine and rather fancy restaurant located in a quiet street east of the Rynek Główny. Dishes on offer include halibut, wild boar served with crispy beetroot chips, fried duck breast with parma ham, and cold morello cherry soup with sorbet.

Cyrano de Bergerac

Sławkowska 26
Expensive and highly-regarded French restaurant in a spacious but cosy cellar in the Old Town. There is a patio for summer dining. World-class French cuisine includes foie gras and various fish dishes, with turbot and mullet on offer; extensive wine list. Worth the price if you can afford it!

Hotel Francuski

Pijarska 13
Big, old-fashioned restaurant in a smart city-centre hotel located opposite the Church of the Holy Trinity. Extensive wine and spirit list. Open until midnight; the elegant, refined, and rather elderly diners look as though they'll probably go to bed much earlier, though.

Hotel Elektor

Corner of sw.Marka and
Szpitalna
Refined, small, expensive restaurant in ultra-smart hotel located opposite the theatre museum. Former diners include King Harald of Norway, the Crown Prince and Princess of Japan, and Queen Elizabeth II, who had lunch here on her visit to Kraków in 1996 (she had veal, with peaches in champagne for dessert). Lots of traditional Polish dishes including plenty of pork, veal and fish, and *żurek*, which is sour rye soup.

Hotel Pod Różą

Floriańska
Smart hotel restaurant serving good but pricey Polish food. Starters include cold beetroot soup; main courses include caviar, pierogi, pork with plum sauce and veal tongue with anchovy sauce.

Wierzynek

Rynek Główny (near Grodska)
Most famous restaurant in Kraków; the food is good, and prices are actually quite reasonable, although you pay partly for the reputation and setting as well the food. Mainly Polish dishes, with duck and fish (especially trout) a speciality. The artwork and the French slant to some of the dishes lend the place a sophisticated air. The upstairs dining area overlooks the main square, but you'll need to book in advance for a table by the window.

Tetmajerowska

Rynek Główny 34
An expensive and refined restaurant serving traditional Polish food in a venue whose interior decoration is by the early twentieth century artist Włodzimierz Tetmajer, after whom the place is named. The cuisine is Polish: dishes include caviar and herrings in cream. Service is exemplary.

Coffee Houses

Kraków's *Mitteleuropa* Austrian heritage means that it still has something of a coffee house culture, rather like other central European cities such as Budapest and Vienna. Today coffee houses *(kawarnia)* come in a number of different forms, from traditional places like *Jama Michalika* on Floriańska, which sells enough variety of food to make it a good place for a meal, to smaller, more off-beat places which sell nothing but coffee (although there are often lots of different varieties of the dark stuff on offer). Besides the *Jama Michalika* there are other former coffee houses which now sell food (such as the Redolfi on the main square) and are nowadays indistinguishable from restaurants. Many hotels have *kawarnia* attached to them which are bland, indifferent places; here, though, are some city-centre coffee houses which are good for spending some time in, drinking, reading and people-watching.

Jama Michalika

This traditional, venerable coffee house on Floriańska, opened in 1895, is always busy with visitors and is a bit of a tourist haunt, but it's the best place to become acquainted with Cracovian coffee house culture. It's a gloomily attractive, atmospheric and cavernous place, old fashioned and refined, and a good refuge away from the bustle of Floriańska street. The Art Nouveau interior, furnishings and stained glass have hardly changed since the days of the Austro-Hungarian Empire. The institution's name means *Michalik's Grotto* (referring to the lack of windows) and for a while it was the venue for a cabaret and revue act known as the Green Balloon, whose songs and puppet shows caused a scandal among polite Cracovian society. The cabaret's chief instigator was Stanisłśaw Przbyszewski who, when he ran out of money, began paying the café's proprietor in artworks – and part of this collection can still be seen. Besides coffee there are savoury snacks, soups, elegant cakes and other pastries and desserts on offer.

Café Botanica

This place on Bracka, just off the main square, offers coffee, cakes and savoury dishes in spacious surroundings decked with plants (both living and plastic).

Demmers

Demmers, on Kanonicza Street, opposite the *Copernicus* hotel, offers a huge variety of teas, plus coffee, although there is little in the way of food on offer. Another Kraków drinking establishment which makes good use of ancient cellars.

Noworolski

Tucked into an arcade in the Sukiennice, this has been a popular café since the nineteenth century. The interior boasts wonderful art-nouveau decoration and the whole place is a throwback to the elegance and sophistication the upper classes enjoyed during the days of the Austro-Hungarian empire. Lots of elegant and fancy cakes and pastries are on offer in a place popular with both tourists and locals, who indulge in appropriately highbrow conversations over newspapers and copious amounts of cigarette smoke.

Redolfi

Slightly gloomy but intimate coffee house and restaurant in a prime position on the main square, overlooking the northern entrance to the Sukiennice. Serves a traditional Polish breakfast (with tomatoes, cottage cheese and horseradishes on offer), but more handy for a quick lunch, with meat and fish dishes (including duck, veal and salmon), and desserts including pancakes.

Shopping

Kraków's medieval wealth was based on trading – as attested to by the large houses of rich merchants that surround the Rynek Główny, and by the opulence of the *Sukiennice*, the grandiose hall where cloth was traded in former times. Nowadays buying and selling is still high on the agenda in Kraków; the Rynek Główny is surrounded by shops selling everything from books and CDs to craftwork from the local area, and many visitors to the city will want to spend time hunting around these places for some distinctive souvenirs to take home with them.

For **food shopping**, there are supermarkets on Szpitalna, opposite the Słowacki theatre; at the corner of Krasińskiego and Zwierzyniecka (the ground floor of the Jubilat department store), due west of Wawel; and in the **Galeria Krakówska**, the enormous shopping centre situated 800m northeast of the Rynek Główny (main entrance on the square by the railway station, with other entrances from Pawia, and from the bus and train stations themselves). A wander through this gleaming glass-and-chrome temple of consumerism provides an enlightening insight into the bold, brash new confidence of post-communist Poland – although the sheen wears off after a bit, and the shopping centre is really like any other anywhere else in the western world. Further out into the city's suburbs there is a Tesco **hypermarket** at the southern end of Kapelanka, around 4km south of the Rynek Główny, which is open 24 hours, and a Géant hypermarket on al.Bora-Komorowskiego in the northern suburbs. For a rather more genuinely Polish experience shopping for food, head for the **Rynek Kleparski**, a maze of stalls located 400m west of the station that sell fresh fruit and vegetable produce, much of it from the local area. The market is on the left side of Warszawska as it heads north from Basztowa. (On Tuesdays and Fridays stalls selling various items such as wickerwork and brooms also open up here.) For **sweets and chocolate**, head for the Wawel Shop at Rynek Główny 33, and for local **cheese and cold meats**, the Pod Aniołami shop at Grodzka 35 sells oszczypek cheese from the Highlands in addition to country-style bread baked in traditional log-fired ovens.

Being a university city, Kraków abounds in **bookshops** – but most of them sell books that are only in Polish. The two main sources for books in English are Empik, on the east side of the Rynek Główny (open 10am-10pm daily) and Massolit at ul.Felicjanek 4, in the southwest of the Old Town (open until 8pm daily). The former store is oriented more towards travel guides and maps, whereas the latter has plenty of Polish literature in translation, as well as many books about Polish history and culture. Both shops have a café. There is also a specialist English-language bookshop, the *American Bookshop*, in the Galeria Krakówska, selling lots of English translations of Polish books. For **CDs** and **DVDs**, which tend to be much cheaper than back home, head for the basement of Empik or the branch of the German electrical store Saturn situated at the north end of the Galeria Krakówska (see above under "food shopping"). The Galeria also has another branch of Empik, on the lower floor in the south end, which sells many CDs and DVDs. **Film and camera** supplies are sold at Empik on the Rynek Główny.

Souvenirs and **arts-and-crafts** items tend to be sold around the Rynek Główny, most particularly in the Sukiennice where stalls do a roaring trade in amber and silver jewellery (much of it made around Poland's Baltic coast), woollen jumpers, wood-carved chess sets from the mountainous Podhale region, wood-carved toys, embroidery (particularly hand-embroidered linen table cloths) and glassware. Other items include painted Easter eggs and walking sticks with axe-like handles that also come from the mountain regions to the south of Kraków. Another place to browse for handmade crafts and souvenirs is Made in Poland at ul.Gołębia 2 – although this place is firmly oriented towards tourists, as its name suggests. The Calik gallery, Rynek Główny 7, is famous for selling **Christmas decorations**. Desa, on ul.Grodzka

2, is an **antique** store selling folk art, furniture and porcelain, aimed more at serious collectors rather than casual tourists. Bear in mind, however, that it is illegal to export from Poland any work of art (including printed books) produced before 1945. (Those who require a licence should apply to the Conservation Department at Kanonicza 24 (☎ 012 431 2545).

Florists congregate around the Mickiewicz statue on the Rynek Główny and even place flowers around the statue on the poet's birthday.

Sport and outdoor recreation

There is a **bowling alley** in the Fantasy Park at al.Pokoju 44 open daily from noon, and **golf courses** in the village of Krzeszowice, west if the city (www.Kraków-valley.com) and at Ochmanów, 19km east of Kraków. (www.Krakówgolf.pl). For **horseriding**, contact the Ewelina Riding Club at Jeżynowa 9 (☎ 012 643 5222). In the village of Kryspinów, due west of the city and immediately south of the airport, there is a **recreational lake** with beaches and windsurfing facilities. Part of the lake has a supervised bathing area.

Football matches are played at the Wisła Stadium on Reymonta and at the Cracovia Stadium on al.Focha. The teams that play at these stadia are, respectively, Wisla Kraków (whose colours are blue, white and red) and Cracovia (red and white). (Cracovia was the team supported by Pope John Paul II and their stadium is named after him.) The teams are bitter rivals and matches tend to attract hooligans (and consequently lots of police in riot gear) and many may find the atmosphere a little forbidding. Men under 30 are required to show ID to get into the stadium. For this reason you should visit the stadium before the match to obtain an ID card (take a photograph and your passport).

Telephones and Fax

Poland's telephone system has hauled itself rapidly out of the Dark Ages and is now reliable and easy to use. You will see plenty of people buzzing around with mobile phones, and you can even rent one for yourself at flash hotels.

Emergency Numbers: Ambulance 999, Fire 998 and Police 997

There are plenty of **public telephones** in the street, hooked up to the international phone network, which are operated using phone cards *(karta telefoniczna)* (there are no public telephones that accept coins). These can be purchased at hotels and *RUCH* street kiosks. The perforated corner of the phone card must be detached before it can be used. The **Telephone Service Centre,** situated in the main post office on Westerplatte, 300m (320 yards) east of the main square, is open 24 hours; use it if you have difficulty getting through or if you want to send a fax. International and internal calls can of course be placed from all hotels – from where phoning is easier, more reliable and *much* more expensive.

Phone calls can also be made from post offices; a call is made from a booth and you pay the cashier when the call is over. Phone calls can also be made from upmarket hotels – though you'll pay a premium, as you would anywhere else in the world. Those with mobile phones will need to ask their operator to switch on their international access facility before they leave home.

Dialling Codes

To call countries abroad from Poland dial the following international access codes: UK-0044, USA-011, Ireland-00353, Canada-001
Omit the first 0 from the area/city code in each case. You may need to wait for the tone to change after dialling the first zero. To call Poland from other countries, dial the following international access codes.
from UK-0048, from USA-01148, from Ireland-01048, from Canada-01148
Omit the first 0 from the area/city code in each case.

Calls within Poland

The code for Kraków is 012. If you are placing city-to-city calls within Poland you should wait after dialling the initial 0 of the area / city code, and continue to dial after the tone has changed. Warsaw numbers have the code 02 for seven digit numbers and 022 for six digit numbers.

Time

Poland runs on Central European Time (CET) – the same as France and Germany. In the summer the time is GMT+2hrs (BST+1) and in winter GMT+1hr. New York time is six hours behind CET. Clocks go forward one hour at the end of March and back one hour at the end of September.

Tourist Information

The main **city tourist office** is a pavilion located amidst the greenery of the Planty, at ul.Szpitalna 25, between the Hotel Polonia and the Słowacki Theatre (see map, p.000). It gives out a good range of information about the city, although you should use different offices if you want information on accommodation or cultural events (see relevant *FactFile* sections). The office is open from 9am-5pm daily; ☎ (012) 432 0110. The main tourist-oriented **websites** are www.Kraków.pl and www.cracow-life.com and www.explore-krakow.com.

A number of **private 'tourist offices'** have sprung up in the city centre, particularly along Floriańska. They mainly organize tours out to Auschwitz, Warsaw and the High Tatras, walking tours around Kraków itself, and offer currency exchange services. These include the Cool Tour Company (www.cooltourcompany.com) which offers off-beat walks around the city centre, Nowa Huta and Kazimierz; and the Tourist Information Office at pl Mariacki 3 (behind the Mariacki Church) which offers hotel reservations, tours and car rental.

Orbis, the state travel agency and tourist office, has a useful branch on the north-eastern side of the Rynek Główny, which is open from 9am to 6pm (2pm on Saturday). They offer local tourist information, details of organized tours to places such as Auschwitz and the Wieliczka salt mine, sightseeing tours of Kraków, currency exchange facilities and internal and international train and bus tickets and information.

Transport

Kraków has an excellent urban public transport system, consisting of buses, trams and taxis, which are cheap, efficient, extensive and fast. Having said this, the centre of Kraków is very compact and the easiest way of getting around is on foot. You are only likely to make extensive use of public transport if you're travelling to the airport, or one of the places described in Chapter 4, or are staying in a far-flung area of the city.

Trams and Buses

These operate on extensive routes, many of which start in the city centre (or near the station) and run into the suburbs; routes and stops are shown very clearly on the recommended map. The tram system runs from around 4.30am to 11pm. At night there are night buses (indicated by route numbers of 600 and over) but no trams.

The same tickets (*bilety*) are used on trams and buses; buy them at *Ruch* kiosks (street-side kiosks which you can find all over the centre of Kraków), or at other selected stalls or hotels where you see the MPK symbol. It is not usually possible to buy tickets on trams and buses themselves. The kiosk opposite the *Polonia* hotel on Basztowa is one of the best places to buy tickets, which are of several types:

Bilet Jednorazowy – a single fare ticket, good for one journey with no changes, so long as you complete your journey within an hour. The ticket must be validated after boarding the tram or bus in one of the on-board punching machines, which stamps the ticket with the time. Large pieces of luggage need their own separate ticket.

Bilet czasownyna 60 minuty – good for unlimited travel over a sixty minute period, starting from when it is validated using the on-board machine. Again, large items of luggage will need a separate ticket.

Bilet dzienny – a one day ticket. Valid from the time of punching until midnight. No separate tickets for luggage.

Bilet tygodniewy – allows a week's unlimited travel. The name of the holder is written on the ticket and in theory ID should be carried when using this ticket. No separate tickets for luggage.

In addition, group and family tickets are also available.

Those under the age of 4 and over 75 travel free of charge. OAPs and children under the age of 14, students and the disabled are entitled to reduced-fare travel but must carry appropriate documents.

Ticket inspectors wear plain clothes but carry photographic identity; they will fine you on the spot if you cannot produce a ticket.

The Kraków Tourist Card allows for unlimited travel on buses and trams in the city and free admission to 32 museums. Cards are valid for 2 or 3 days. For more information and details of where the card can be purchased (mostly hotels and tourist offices) go to www.krakowcard.com.

Taxis

Taxis are plentiful but not particularly cheap; make sure the driver turns on the meter when you get in. There is an initial charge of around 70 zł and after that a charge of around half that per kilometre (between 11pm and 5am there is a fifty per cent price hike). There are taxi ranks at the junction of Sienna and Westerplatte, on plac Szczepańska (the closest rank to the Rynek Główny), outside the railway station, and on pl. Dominikańska. Any hotel will telephone for a taxi if you ask them to – or contact the following firms direct:

City Taxi	☎ 266 6444
Express Taxi	☎ 644 4111
Krak Taxi	☎ 267 6767

National Rail and Bus Systems

Poland has an extensive, cheap (but not particularly fast) system of trains and buses which reach every corner of this comparatively large country. The best place to arrange national and international bus and train **tickets** is the office of the state travel organisation, Orbis, on Rynek Glówny. The queues at railway and bus stations tend to be long, and few personnel dealing with internal tickets are likely to speak English.

Internal and international trains use the **main train station**, Kraków Główny, a Habsburg era-building located ten minutes' walk north from the Rynek Główny (see map, page 000). Some trains use Plaszów in addition to, or instead of, Główny. Plaszów is in the southern suburbs of the city and a nuisance to get to by bus; use a taxi, or a local train from Główny. The **train service** is operated by PKP, Polish State Railways, which operate four types of train – Intercity (IC, marked in red on timetables, with compulsory seat reservations and more expensive fares than other trains); Express (*Ekspresowy*, also marked in red and also requiring compulsory seat reservations); fast trains (*pospieszny*); and normal trains (*osobowy*, marked in black on timetables). Departures are marked on yellow posters and indicator boards headed *odjazdy* and arrivals are marked on white posters and indicator boards headed *przyjazdy*. Look out for the words *kursuje* or *nie Kursuje* next to train times, followed by dates – meaning the train does or does not run at those times. (Other Polish words you might need are *peron*, platform, and is *przechowalnia bagażu* – the left-luggage office). Train travel is comparatively cheap, whichever class of train you use, and you might want to travel first class *(pierwsza klasa)* even if you never do back home, particularly as trains tend to be very crowded. Ticketing facilities at Kraków Główny are computerized and some information staff speak a little English. However, train information and tickets are easier to get hold of at the Orbis office in central Kraków.

Bus and coach services are operated by PKS, the Polish National Bus Company, and by private bus companies such as Komfort Bus, whose vehicles are much more comfortable than those of PKS. The recently-opened **main bus station,** the Dworzec PKS, is awkwardly located to the east of the train station on Wita Stwosza; the best way to get there on foot from the town centre is to head to the lowest floor of the Galeria Krakówska, the enormous shopping complex in front of the railway station, walk right through it to the far end, and then to follow the signs to the *Dworzec Autobusowy*. Some local buses (mostly minibuses) do not use the main bus station but instead operate from a scruffy terminal on Pawia, 200m due west of Główny Railway station. You are likely to come here for services to Wadowice and Wielicka (see chapter Four).

Travelling to Kraków by Air

Kraków is served by **John Paul II International Airport** which is located at Balice, 15km (10 miles) west of the city. It's small and easy to use and was completely overhauled for the visit of Pope John Paul II to the city in 1995. The airport is linked to the city by taxis (40-70 zł, journey time: 20 mins) and by two bus routes, the 192 and 692 (the latter a night bus), both of which can be picked up in the city centre from outside the Hotel Cracovia or from outside the main city-centre LOT office on Basztowa (look for Port Lotniczy–Airport). Journey time is around 35 minutes. (Another bus, the 208, also runs from the airport into Kraków, but its terminus is at Nowy Kleparz, around 1200m north of the city centre.) In addition, a fast train (journey time 15 minutes) links the main railway station in Kraków with Balice station (fare: 4 zł) which is 200m from the airport terminal (there is a free shuttle bus between the terminal and Balice station). There are around two rail services per hour, operating between 4am and midnight.

Flights from the British Isles

British Airways (☎ 0870 850 9850 in UK; www.ba.com) operates a direct, non-stop flight from London (Gatwick) to Kraków most days (journey time 2½ hours), and **Aer Lingus** (☎ 0818 365 000 in Ireland; www.aerlingus.com) operates direct, non-stop flights between Dublin and Kraków around five times per week (journey time 2 hours

50 minutes). **LOT Polish Airlines** do not run any flights out of Kraków to the UK or Ireland but operate flights from Heathrow, Dublin and Manchester to Warsaw, which will connect with one of the 6-7 daily flights from Warsaw to Kraków (45-55 mins).

Note that a number of **internet travel companies**, such as www.expedia.co.uk, www.travelocity.co.uk or www.lastminute.com will be able to organize a flights-and-accommodation package to Kraków, which might work out cheaper than booking hotels and flights separately. In addition, companies such as Polorbis or Polish regency Tours (☎ 020 8992 8866; www.polish-travel.com) can organize weekend breaks to Kraków and other Polish cities.

British Airways office in Kraków: ☎ (012) 285 5033 at Balice Airport
Aer Lingus can be contacted in Poland at their Warsaw office on ☎ (022) 626 8402.

In addition to the services operated by LOT, British Airways and Aer Lingus, a number of no-frills, **low-cost airlines** have opened up routes between Kraków and airports in the UK and Ireland in recent years. These include centralwings, a Polish owned and operated budget airline (which is an offshoot of LOT), in addition to familiar names on the low-frills travel scene such as Ryanair and easyJet. Although phone numbers have been given for these it is always cheaper and more convenient to book these flights over the internet. Check that when you see Kraków listed as a destination, airlines mean Kraków-Balice airport, and not the airport at Katowice, around 50km to the west, which handles some flights that label themselves as heading for Kraków. Routes are notoriously fickle, but at the time of writing the following airlines were running direct non-stop flights into Kraków from cities in England, Scotland and the Irish Republic: SkyEurope (☎ 0905 722 2747; www.skyeurope.com). Services to Kraków from Birmingham, Dublin, Manchester (in Kraków ☎[012] 290 6770). easyJet (☎ 0905 821 0905; www.easyjet.com). Services to Kraków from Bristol, Liverpool and London Luton (in Kraków ☎[012] 639 3428). centralwings (www.centralwings.com). Services to Kraków from Cork and London Gatwick (in Kraków ☎ [012] 639 3424). Ryanair (☎ 0871 246 0000; in UK, ☎ 01609 7800 in Ireland; www.ryanair.com) Services to Kraków from Dublin, East Midlands, Glasgow, Liverpool, London Stansted and Shannon . Jet2.com (☎ 020 7170 0737; www.jet2.com) Services to Kraków from Leeds/Bradford and Newcastle.

Flights from the USA and Canada

The only location in North America served by direct, non-stop LOT flight from Kraków is Chicago, with services twice weekly. Not surprisingly, there's a better choice of flights between North America and Warsaw, with LOT flying from New York, Chicago and Toronto to the Polish capital. Contact details for LOT are on p.155. No North American operators serve Warsaw at present, and unless you fly LOT a flight from North America to Warsaw will involve a change of planes in a European airport.

Travelling to Kraków: surface routes from the UK

By Bus

Eurolines (☎ 0870 514 3219; www.eurolines.com) run four weekly services from London (Victoria Coach Station) to Kraków (Central Bus Terminal, next to Kraków-Główny railway station). The journey time is 30 hours (with frequent stops). Return flights start from around £70.

By Train

Travelling by train from London to Kraków takes a minimum of 30 hours. Which trains and routes you take depends partly on which time of year you're travelling – services are more frequent in June-September. The return fare from London, with couchette, is around £280.

From London you will travel to Brussels (via *Eurostar* through the Channel Tunnel) and then via Köln (Cologne), Hannover, Berlin and then Warsaw or Wrocław/Katowice. The bulk of the journey is best done on the nightly train which leaves Cologne in the early evening (with plenty of time to get there from London via Brussels) and arrives in Warsaw the next morning. The fastest trains between Warsaw and Kraków take 2 hrs 30min, but reservations are compulsory; try to arrange for these reservations, as well as couchette (sleeping berth) tickets, when you book from London. There are also direct trains from Berlin to Kraków which travel via Wrocław and Katowice (more direct than via Warsaw), and which take eight hours (one overnight).

You can arrange train times to see something of cities *en route* such as Brussels, Cologne, Berlin or Warsaw. For detailed information on timings consult the *Thomas Cook European Timetable*, published monthly and available from Thomas Cook travel agencies, through bookshops and in reference sections of large UK public libraries (or online at www.thomascookpublishing.com).

For information on tickets and fares, contact Rail Europe on ☎ 08705 848848 or go to their website, www.raileurope.co.uk, or visit their travel centre at 178 Piccadilly. London W1. You might also find the London offices of German Railways (☎ 08702 435363) useful when making travel arrangements. They also maintain an excellent website, www.deutsche-bahn.co.uk, with ticket-booking facilities and comprehensive timetables covering the whole of Europe.

Orbis

There are offices of Orbis, the Polish state travel organisation, which deals with accommodation, flights and group and individual travel, at:

14 Elizabeth Street
London SW1W 9RB
☎ 020 7730 6872

342 Madison Avenue
New York, NY 10173
☎ 212 867 5011

Polish Tourist Offices

Branches of the polish national tourist office, which give out brochures and other tourist
information, are at:

Level 3
West Gate House
West Gate
London W5 1YT
☎ 08700 675010
www.visitpoland.org

5 Marine View Plaza
Hoboken
NJ 07030
☎ 201 420 9910
www.polandtour.org

LOT - Polish Airlines ticket offices and contact information

In Kraków:

LOT-Polish Airlines ticket offices
Basztowa 15
☎ 0801 703 703
fax (012) 422 6683
Open: 9am-6pm weekdays,
9am-3pm Sat.

In the UK and Ireland:

Level 8, 414 Chiswick High Road,
London W4 5TF
☎ 0870 414 0088
Reservations and information on
☎ 0845 6010949

Room 124
Terminal 2
London Heathrow Airport
☎ (020) 8745 7270
☎ (020) 8745 2004 (ticket desk)
Globeground Ticket Desk
Manchester Airport
☎ (0161) 869 489 3186
fax (0161) 489 3767

ACA International Terminal
Building
Dublin Airport
☎ 1890 35956

In the USA and Canada:

333 North Michigan Avenue
suite 921
Chicago
Illinois 60601

Terminal 5
O'Hare Airport
☎ (773) 686 7515/6

500 Fifth Avenue, Suite 408
New York 10110
☎ (212) 869 0970
or ☎ (212) 223 0593 for callers outside
NYC area

Sales and reservations in USA:
☎ 1 800 223 0593

Clarica Centre
Centre Tower, 10th Floor
3300 Bloor Street West
Suite 3080
Toronto M8X 2X3
☎(416) 236 4242
or (905) 676 0866
at Lester B Pearson Airport

Website:

LOT have an English-language website which can be used
for buying tickets by credit
card; tickets are then mailed to any country in the world.
www.lot.com

Index

Index

Published in the UK by
Landmark Publishing Ltd,
Ashbourne Hall, Cokayne Ave, Ashbourne, Derbyshire, DE6 1EJ
☎ (01335) 347349 Fax: (01335) 347303 e-mail: landmark@clara.net
website: www.landmarkpublishing.co.uk

Published in the USA by
Hunter Publishing
222 Clematis Street, West Palm Beach FL 33401 USA
☎ 001 561 835 2022 e-mail: michael@hunterpublishing.com

3rd Edition
ISBN 13: 978-1-84306-308-7
ISBN 10: 1-84306-308-5

British Library Cataloguing in Publication Data: a catalogue record for this book is available from the British Library.

Print: Cromwell Press, Trowbridge

Cartography & Design: Sarah Labuhn

Front cover: Wawel Cathedral

Back cover, top: Rynek Główny - the city's main square

Back cover, bottom: Wawel, seen from the south bank of the Wisła river

Picture Credits

Panos Pictures: Back cover, top & 94

Hanna Komarnicka: 31R, 46

Hedley Alcock OBE: 25, 58, 62B, 95

Sarah Labuhn: Cover, 6, 19B, 23R, 54, 91

All other photographs are supplied by the authors